HOW
YOU
ALWAYS
MEANT
to
PARENT

Brian Housman

randall house

Printed in the United States of America

13-ISBN 9780892656745

Dedicated to Bailey and Ashlan

One of the greatest joys of my life has been walking with you through childhood and adolescence to see you become the man and woman that you are today. Your mom and I could not be more proud of the way that you honor the Lord in all that you do. You are a gift to our lives beyond anything we could have fathomed.

Hold on to the pattern of wholesome teaching you learned from me—a pattern shaped by the faith and love that you have in Christ Jesus. Through the power of the Holy Spirit who lives within us, carefully guard the precious truth that has been entrusted to you.

2 Timothy 1:13 &14

Table of Contents

Introduction

The list of life skills and tasks you have taught your child to master is endless. All it takes is a cursory glance through your family scrapbook to be reminded of the life lessons you have taught. There is the picture of her awkwardly holding a tiny baby spoon as you showed her how to feed herself. There is the one of her proudly showing off the shirt she buttoned up all by herself (after you showed her countless times). Don't forget the snapshot of him proudly pointing in the toilet to show you what "big boys" do. As they grew older you have had, or will have, the joy of teaching them to tie their own shoes, ride a bike through the woods, recover from a broken heart, and fill out a job application.

One overarching lesson starts in childhood and continues through the rest of your life. It is the journey of helping your child discover the God who made them and loves them beyond your own capacity. It is a process that starts in simple ways of showing your child how God wants to know them. It involves walking through the glory and the gore of the teenage years with them. Finally, it culminates with you setting them free to be used by God to make a difference in the world. It begins with a process in which you got the privilege of being the one to help your child discover a wonder and excitement for the God who made them.

In eons past, God had already determined to knit you and your child together to be a family. He knew that your children's best chance of discovering who God is was to put them under your shepherding care. Is that not amazing? God willfully and intentionally chose you to be the one to teach them about God's love. If you choose, you can have a loving relationship with them that lasts a lifetime. You can choose to have something that many parents may never experience—a relationship with your children built on honor, respect, and dignity as you grow in a spiritual relationship with God.

Everything you have done, or meant to do, in your child's life so far has been part of the spiritual process you are in together. Each day, you have made choices to jump in, for better or worse, to play the role of spiritual mentor to your child. Or you made a choice to do very little. Either way, your level of spiritual engagement has always been your choice.

That doesn't mean that your children's spiritual maturity is solely up to you. You can be completely engaged in their lives, but in the end, they could still choose not to honor God or connect with Him. In the end, your child's spiritual health comes down to his or her own choices. This is particularly true as they grow into teenagers. They will have to own the choices they make for themselves.

This graph shows how your role and your child's role work hand in hand.

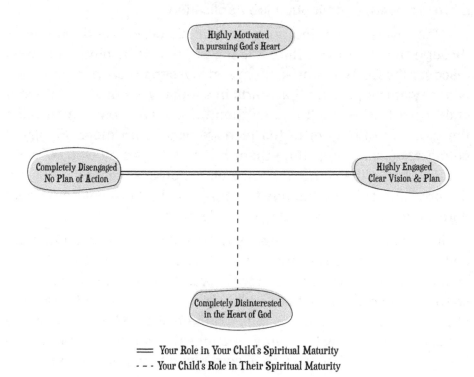

== Your Role in Your Child's Spiritual Maturity
- - - Your Child's Role in Their Spiritual Maturity

Your actions in your child's spiritual development lands somewhere on the horizontal line of the graph between completely disengaged with no plan and highly engaged with a clear vision. If you have actively been walking with your child to help shape their understanding of God and learning to find their place in His world, then reading this book will reinforce what you have already been doing. On the other hand, if you are like many of us as we begin parenting, then you are somewhere closer to still trying to figure out your game plan and choose what the next step are going to be in your child's life.

Your children's role in their own spiritual growth can be marked somewhere on the vertical line of the graph. The more self-engaging they are with God, the easier it will be to lead them as the two of you walk on a spiritual journey together. There will be times in the teen years when your child is laser-focused on their walk with Christ and you will feel like things could not get any better. Likewise, there may be times when they appear to be drifting like a boat without a sail. During these times they may feel less open to discussing spiritual matters with you.

As you look at where each of you land on the chart, you might feel like you're both about to fall off the bottom left-hand side of the page. That is okay. You might see yourselves surging toward the upper right-hand of the graph. That too is okay. Regardless of where you are, this is just to give you a starting place for today.

You may be a parent who has tried and tried to help your child discover Christ, but for years now all you have seen in return is a hardened heart. I know this makes your heart heavy to see no fruit from your effort. No matter what has happened so far, keep reminding yourself that your job is to love and lead. The Holy Spirit's job is to convict and save.

This was my own mother's experience. From the time my brother and I were born, she took us to church. We heard the same messages, went to the same Vacation Bible Schools, and attended the same youth camps. Early on as a child, I remember asking Jesus to come into my heart and live with me forever. My brother's response to the gospel was just the opposite. He ran from God and wanted nothing to do with spiritual matters. Yet, years later in his early 20s, something clicked. He surrendered his life to Christ and there was a radical transformation in his life. It all happened in God's timing, not our mom's timing.

Regardless of where your child is on the graph, God has a plan and a big part of that plan starts with you. Before you dive into the principles in the book of learning to leave a spiritual legacy in your child's life, I have three thoughts of encouragement for you.

First, the great news about being in a spiritual journey with your child is that it starts today. You can't fix what you did not do in the past. You can only move forward and choose to be more spiritually engaged and intentional for *today*. At some point you may feel the need to apologize to your children for not being a spiritual leader to them, but that doesn't mean you need to rehash all of your mistakes as a parent. Your past failures do not equate to future experiences. That is not the way God works with us. Whether your failures as a parent were long ago or yesterday, God wants your focus on Him and how He desires to redeem those failures. Take a look at these words from 2 Corinthians 12:9 and embrace them as your own:

> But he said to me, "My grace is sufficient for you, for my power is made perfect in weakness. Therefore I will boast all the more gladly about my weaknesses, so that Christ's power may rest on me."

If you are a parent who feels as if you have royally blown things with your children, then the good news is you are the perfect vessel for God's power. As a matter of fact, the only qualification for being the kind of person in whom God's power is made perfect is that YOU MUST BE WEAK. Recognizing when you've crashed and burned is the first step to His power resting on you.

Second, your child desires for you to engage him on a spiritual level. The typical teenager doesn't know how to express gratitude to their parent for all the parent does in their life. I have prayed with my children dozens of times, but it is not like they pause to say "thanks" after each time. We have had countless conversations about everything from moral boundaries and academic struggles to serving others in their walk with Christ. Not once has my son said, "Thanks for talking with me about girls," or has my daughter said, "I appreciate you understanding when my friends were being jerks." But I know they both greatly appreciate it—even more so, their actions show me they value time with me.

When your children were born, God hard wired your heart to theirs. It is the most important human connection they have in their lives. When they were young, they asked you a thousand questions, loved cuddling with you and wanted you to play with them because you uniquely filled a need in their lives. As your child grows older, they may be less verbal with their words of appreciation, but they still feel the same way when you spend time with them.

Don't let the "cold shoulder," rolling eyes, or deep sigh fool you. There are times when your teen would rather be with you than any-one else. In a 2007 MTV study, teenagers were asked what one thing makes them feel the happiest in life.[1] More teenagers said spending time with their family than anything else. Would you believe that 72 percent of teens prefer spending time with their families?

My final thought of encouragement is not to get overwhelmed with the principles you and I explore in this book. Starting a spiritual journey with your child begins with taking a first step, not with try-ing to master all things the first day. Take the content in bite-sized pieces. If it starts feeling too heavy, convicting, or confusing for you, put it down for a few days and then come back later.

In some regards, this book may raise more questions for you than it answers. That is okay. The things we discuss may not easily fit systematically within every family's structure. The goal is not to give you specifics of how to handle every scenario with your teen-ager, but instead to give you some broad principles to incorporate spiritual truths. The application or implementation of those principles will look a little different from family to family. As we follow them within the context God gave us, things will work out. Every family is different. Additionally, the application may change during different seasons of your relationship with your teen.

Chapter 1

Recognizing God's Process

It all started when you got the big news you were having a baby. Suddenly, and without any real knowledge of how to raise a baby, you went into overdrive trying to get everything ready for when you would bring them home. Your life with your children has been a series of processes one after the other. You read books, bought clothes, painted the room, went to numerous doctor visits, and became quite the authority on car seats. In no time at all, you were prepared to talk birthing methods and sleep schedules with the best of them. Your special bundle was still six months away, yet you had already worked the process to be ready.

Much too soon for you, your newbie became a rug rat and was crawling into everything. You got busy and shortened the cords on the mini blinds, covered all of the electrical outlets, installed rubber bumpers on coffee table corners, and put child-proof latches on the cabinets. If you are like most parents, you probably went overboard in bringing your home up to safety standards of which even OSHA would approve, but you had heard there was a process and you were sure to work every step in it.

The same thing happened when your child learned to walk, ride a bike, write the alphabet, swim in a pool, and study for tests in school. One process after another, you walked through with your child. At each junction, you were right there beside your child helping him or her face each challenge, master the skills necessary, and succeed.

Then the teenage years hit. Hard. In your child's opinion, you went from being a Zen Master of all things related to life and morphed into their own real world version of Homer Simpson. This child who once was the source of such joy and affirmation in your life now causes you to perpetually live with fear, frustration, or failure—the three "F"s every one of us has experienced as a parent. For about ten years, these "F"s dig their claws into your skin and hang on like a bad friend who never pays for his own lunch.

Recognizing the Three "F"s

Early on you may have had a rock-solid confidence in your abilities and an appreciation that your child needs you for pretty much everything. Then, in what seems like an overnight flip of a switch, you began to develop a complete and utter insecurity about parenting. You went from being a gourmet chef of peanut butter and jelly, a healer of all scrapes, and a skilled negotiator…to a parent paralyzed by fear. You traded in your expertise and excitement about parenting in exchange for fear and failure.

Don't worry. You are not alone. For most parents, confidence is replaced with some level of fear during the teen years. Fear of outside influences, fear of your teenager's future, fear of screwing up your teen, and fear of your child finding out about your past—these are the toxins that keep us awake at night. One dad with two teenage daughters told me, "I get so terrified sometimes that I feel like I want to barricade the front door and cut all the lines coming to the house." It is easy to get so distracted by the "what if's" that you do not get to enjoy everyday moments with your teen.

If your default is not fear, then perhaps it's failure. Your own failure, your teen's failure, your spouse's failure—take your pick. It is remarkably easy for us to become immobilized by failures as parents. The older your teen gets, the list of things that make you feel like less and less of a success as a parent grows longer. At the end of the week, the checklist of your failures can threaten to rob you of any joy.

☑ I don't check their phones enough.

☑ I don't make sure they get enough sleep.

☑ I can't keep up with all of their friends.

☑ I can't control my temper when responding to their moods.

☑ I forget to affirm their efforts.

☑ I forget to check up on their homework and grades.

☑ I don't pray with them anymore.

☑ I don't make time for significant conversations.

Some responsibilities are more important than others, but big or small, failure in the little things seems to paralyze parents. Maybe things didn't go so well with you and your child yesterday. Maybe things haven't been good for a while now. Regardless, it does not mean you have to choke down a big dose of guilt at the start of each day. The problem with feeling like a failure as a parent is that it does not easily go away. As long as you want it to, failure is willing to stick with you like an invisible rash that never leaves your side. It is more than happy to remind you that you do not make the cut as a parent.

By the time children are 11 or 12 years old, many parents describe an overriding feeling of frustration. Somewhere along the way, the wheels seemed to come off the relationship. You begrudgingly embraced the role as your child's personal police officer or secretary. You are always at the ready to either reign in her bad behavior or make sure all of her tasks are completed. You go to bed tired and tense, wondering if it will always be this way. It feels as if the only words you hear from your tween's mouth are "I already knew that," "I don't want to," or "You don't understand." With a long face, one parent of a tween commented to me, "This is just not fun anymore."

Let's be honest. Every one of us has struggled with the three "F"s at some point. Whether being slapped around by them from time to time or being owned by them, we all know what it's like to feel fear, failure, and frustration. The scary thing is when you start believing that this is the way it is supposed to be—as if this is as good as it will ever get with your teenager.

If this is you, I want you to hear this truth. This IS NOT the relationship that God intends for you to have with your child for the long term. He has something far more dynamic, life-breathing, and transformative in mind for you. When God gave you the blessing of being a parent, He meant for it to be an experience that would change both your life and your child's life in order to make you both more like Christ Himself. He gave your child to you so you could both learn a deeper knowledge *of Him*, a greater dependency *on Him*, and a truer spiritual intimacy *with Him*.

Here is one of the keys. Here is the reason most parents live with fear, failure, and frustration. Here is why many parents give up and believe this is as good as it gets. We have forgotten part of the process...and it is all about God. God's desire is for us to know Him and enjoy Him forever. Listen to how the apostle Paul describes the relationship of all things to God.

> *For from him and through him and for him are all things. To him be the glory forever! Amen* (Romans 11:36).

God created, and it came back to Him. God blesses, and it comes back to Him. God works through all things, and it comes back to Him. God allows failure or disappointment, and it comes back to Him. All of life is intended to be connected to the One who makes all things for His glory.

His desire is for you and your child to be connected *to* Him and follow Him together. When this happens parenting becomes exciting, redemptive, and affirming. Don't get me wrong, parenting is still hard work—probably the hardest thing you will ever do. But when you are developing a dependency on God, you are helping your child to discover the wonder of God. When you are walking with God together, it is rewarding beyond words. Then the small stuff that leads to fear, failure, and frustration doesn't seem nearly as strangling.

Cooler Heads Prevail

Several years ago when I was just getting started in a speaking ministry, we learned the joy of living on less. I mention the joy, but in all honesty, it wasn't always fun. It was a major adjustment to our budget as we created a new ministry for families from scratch. Somewhere in the midst of our many road trips from one speaking engagement to the next, the air conditioning went out in our family van. This might not have been so bad if we lived in Canada. Instead, we lived in Memphis, Tennessee—the humidity capital of America. From mid-May until October it is a constant, sweaty 90-degree plus.

Because of our tight finances, I decided I could fix the air conditioning myself. It was either pay someone else two thousand dollars or figure it out myself. On one hand, I knew nothing about repairing a vehicle's cooling system, but I also knew if I had the right tools, followed the right steps, and had enough time, I could figure it out.

My plan of attack was borderline obsessive-compulsive. I spent several weeks getting advice from anyone I ran into who had ever worked on cars. I went to my local Toyota dealership and had them print me a schematic of the entire A/C system. I spent hours in online forums about Toyota Siennas. I got second and third opinions from other mechanics. I watched every YouTube video I could find on air condition repair for my vehicle. Finally, the day came that I wheeled our van into our garage for amateur surgery.

With much fear, I reached my hands into parts of my vehicle I had never ventured into before. I started taking out bolts, removing screws, and disconnecting cables. Before long, I had the bumper, the condenser, the A/C compressor, and all the belts taken off our minivan. Each time I took off another piece, I took a picture of where it came from and then laid it out on the floor in what started looking like a life-size automobile version of the board game *Operation*.

All of the work, planning, and stress was worth it in the end. After hours and hours of reassembly, my wife flipped the switch to experience cool air again in our family van. Sure it would have been quicker and much easier to take the vehicle in to a repair garage, but I wanted the satisfaction of knowing I could do it. Cool air never felt so...well, cool.

Parenting a teenager is much the same way. It can feel terrifying to start tinkering with your kid's life, all the while thinking, "I'm going to break something here and not know how to put it back together again." There will be many times you feel as if you are not seeing any change in your tween's life. But spiritual maturity in your teenager does not happen overnight and it won't happen by accident. This is a long haul, heavy lifting, midnight-hours type of investment you are making in your teen's life. Just like with my van's air conditioner, there is a process you have to go through when it comes to parenting teens. It is a process that starts when they are young and carries through each day of their lives.

Keeping the End Game in Mind

Before we take a look at the "steps" to you being a spiritual leader in your child's life, you have to ask yourself what is really at stake. What is the end game for your teenager's life? If you try to lead them and parent them without answering this question first, you may not have a clear goal in mind. How do you know what victories to celebrate or what disciplines and lifestyles to work on next? How do you help them deal with failure if there is no end game?

Let's say that your son is a naturally gifted athlete. "He's got the goods," a coach might say. Through hard work, discipline, and good coaching, he starts to develop the right skill set to be a starting running back. You spend hours teaching him perseverance and dedication. Being with other players helps him understand teamwork and loyalty. His coaches show him how to move his body in order to avoid tackles and to maneuver his hands in order to protect the ball. In everyone's estimation, he has what it takes to be a great football player. Now imagine if no one ever told him that the ultimate goal is to get the ball into the end zone. While in the game he gives his full effort, but once he gets past the defender he starts running around like he is in a game of keep away—running back and forth across the field, but never advancing the ball. What if no one told him the end game is to score?

A similar phenomenon happens to us as parents. Believe me, I am right in the thick of this with you. It is too easy to respond only to what you see in front of you when your child is doing something wrong without first thinking through what the end game is for their life. When your daughter makes a bad grade, you want her to try harder. When she talks back to you, you want her to show you respect. When your son picks on a sibling, you want them to stop fighting. Our default mode in parenting becomes behavior modification.

Don't hit. Don't yell. Be nice. Do your homework. Turn off the TV. Listen to me. I see wrong behavior and just want it to stop. We have all done it. I have relied on behavior modification many times myself. When I come home tired from work to find my kids arguing, what I want most in the moment is peace and quiet. Before I can even think about it, I instinctively belt out, "Just stop! Go to your rooms." Then the house is quiet, but my children are not any closer to being in harmony with one another than they were minutes earlier. If someone walked into our home, they might think, "Wow, what a quiet and peaceful home." In reality there is still no lasting peace; rather, there is merely an irritated father barking orders to get his way.

When your teen is completely respectful toward you, it doesn't automatically mean that his heart is like Christ. If your teen is a good citizen, it doesn't mean that she is growing in spiritual maturity. Things may look good on the outside, but the heart may be far from God. A stereotypical mother from past generations may have tweaked her child's cheeks and asserted, "I just want you to be a good boy!" Effective parents are not as concerned with "good" behavior as they are with godliness. Christlikeness can be vastly different than a strict adherence to good morals or good behavior.

Of course, we all agree that right behavior is necessary, but we also recognize that behavior can be deceiving. Thinking back to your own adolescence, you probably could identify the underlying game in your home early on. Perhaps doing what your mom expected or doing the right thing in front of your dad would result in you getting whatever you wanted. Any child knows that living up to the right kind of behavior two weeks before Christmas promises a full bounty under the tree. When mom has a headache or dad is agitated, it is not the right moment to ask to attend a sleepover or receive a raise in allowance. The game was all about right behavior or manipulating the moment.

You can probably see this in your own kids as well. Your children know which parent to go to for certain results. If they want to go to a sleepover, they go to mom. If they want a raise in allowance, they go to dad. Whether the request is to stay up late, go out to dinner, or any number of other privileges, your kids know who to ask in order to have the best chance of getting what they want. They figure out which performance on their part will achieve the best outcome with no concern for integrity or character. Surely, behavior alone cannot be what God has in mind for the way life is to work best.

What Do They Believe?

Instead of being distracted by better and better performance, perhaps it is time to take a step back to see where your child's behavior comes from. Teenagers don't make decisions in a vacuum. While they can be impulsive at times, by and large their behavior comes from their internal belief system. You will rarely, if ever, see a teenager make a belief-based decision that impacts behavior without being able to tie it directly to a personal understanding of how life is supposed to work.

Your teen is the same way. He has developed a set of beliefs about life. He is learning about dating, marriage, work ethics, the role of money, friendship, and faith—the list goes on and on. Whether positive or negative, he is forming his understanding, or his worldview, of life. His worldview is basically his own personal belief system based on prior experiences, observations, and instruction within his environment. As his parent, you are the greatest influence on his beliefs, but other factors play a role as well—such as media, his school, his church, pop culture, and his friends. Whatever behavior you see through him is simply an outward manifestation of his internal belief system. He is acting on what he believes to be true about how life works.

While it's true that teenagers can be impulsive, they typically know exactly why they are doing what they are doing. Unfortunately, too often we as parents don't know why teenagers do what they do. We end up parenting as a reaction to bad behavior instead of taking the time to understand our child's belief system.

I graduated from a public high school back in 1988. If you were a teen back in that time, I'm sure you remember the "Just Say No" Campaign[1]. First Lady Nancy Reagan spearheaded it in 1982. In middle school and high school, we sat through assemblies where we heard from ex-drug dealers, rappers, athletes, and law enforcement officials who told us all to just say no to drugs and alcohol. Politicians spent over $500 million tax dollars during that time on school programs, literature, and ad campaigns telling students to say "no" to drugs and alcohol. Unfortunately, there is little evidence that the campaign changed the way we looked at drugs or the amount of alcohol our peers consumed. Nancy Reagan's campaign was well-intentioned, but in the end the government created a program that merely addressed bad behavior without stopping to understand what teenagers believed in the first place.[1]

As a parent, your teenager's belief system is a much better starting place. Instead of harping on bad behavior, take a step back and try to figure out what your teenager actually believes. When you impact their belief system, the bad behavior will usually take care of itself. This is where Jesus started with his own followers. In John 14:15, Jesus basically said to his disciples, "If you love me, you will keep my commands." (HCSB) He did not say, "Go do what I say, and somewhere along the way you'll start to love me." He knew it was all about their hearts—their deeply held beliefs. If they believed the right things about Jesus, then their obedience would flow from it.

After Jesus was resurrected, He appeared to Peter. This is the same guy that denied he even knew Jesus a few days earlier. It could have been an awkward moment, but that wasn't what Jesus had in mind. "Peter, do you love me?" was the simple question Jesus had for Peter. No doubt, Peter felt humiliated and embarrassed standing in front of Jesus. Peter responded, "Yes, Lord. You know I love you." This same conversation happened three times. After Peter gave the same response a third time, Jesus replies, "Then feed my sheep." It is not until Jesus spends time alone with Peter discerning the heart questions, that He finally gives Peter a command to act on.

I remember a time when my children were in elementary school and were both doing schoolwork in the living room. Out of nowhere I heard my son yell, "Ow, why did you do that?" That was my cue, of course. So, I interrupted their homework to find out what happened. Bailey insisted, "She threw a stapler and hit me in the head!"

We have a pretty lively household, but this was clearly out-of-bounds behavior even for my children. I knew this was a perfect opportunity to address a behavior issue from a belief standpoint. On a more stressful day, I might have responded with anger or guilt without changing anything more than behavior, but this time was different. I asked Ashlan to go to her room for a few minutes to cool off while I attended to my son's claim. I didn't see any blood, bumps, or bruises, so I am thinking that the Academy Award acting moment may not be as big as he was making it.

Me: Okay, so tell me what happened.

Bailey: Well, I was just sitting here doing my homework and Ashlan threw a stapler and hit me.

Me (thinking that might not be the whole story): Well, tell me about what has been happening after school today.

Bailey: I finished up all of my schoolwork really fast today. (This is unusual.) And then I said, "I'm done with all my work and I've got nothing else to do today." Then for no reason Ashlan threw a stapler and hit me in the head

Now, I could understand a bit more of what happened and why. Homework usually comes easily for Bailey who is a very quick learner, while Ashlan does well academically, but struggles a little more. However, on a typical day, my son is slow to finish his schoolwork, preferring to stretch out the time, while my daughter is usually focused and driven to complete her work quickly so she can go hang out with friends. As I knock on Ashlan's bedroom door, I can guess how the next conversation will go.

Me: Hey, Sweetie, are you having a hard time with schoolwork today?

Ashlan (pouting): YES!

Me: Tell me about what happened after school.

Ashlan (cringing): Well, I did really bad on a quiz today.

Me (knowing that she has probably been comparing herself to her brother and feeling like she doesn't measure up): How did that make you feel about your brother?

Ashlan: Well, it makes me mad because he always does good on tests, and I don't ever do as good.

This is not an accurate representation of how Ashlan usually sees herself, so I know that one of her core beliefs about who she is in Christ has been challenged. On a child's level, she is defining who she is based on her performance, and I have to help her see that is not what we value in her. So I continued the conversation, reminding her of how she is fearfully and wonderfully made according to Psalm 139 and building on other positive things we know God has built into her personality until I saw her face begin to soften with relief. Then, I continued to address her previous behavior.

> Me: Hey, let's back up a minute. Tell me something. After school on most days, what is it you usually like about your brother?
>
> Ashlan (grudgingly and after much thought): I like it when he has friends over and he lets me hang out with them, too.
>
> Me (affirming her comment): Well, that's good, isn't it? He can be really nice to you when he wants to, can't he? Do you think it helps him want to treat you better or worse when you throw staplers at him?
>
> Ashlan (starting to smile in spite of her situation): Probably worse.
>
> Me: What might you need to do now in order to make things right with your brother? I think he might not feel good right now about letting you hang out with him and his friends when you treat him that way.

I left her alone for a few minutes and waited to see what would happen. After a while, she came out and handed her brother a card she had made for him. I never once had to say, "By the way, don't throw staplers." Her heart had already begun to change by that point. And when the heart is changed, right behavior follows.

As parents, instead of addressing only good behavior or bad behavior, we can begin to address the heart. Our culture is big on praising children. We try to develop their self-esteem so they will believe in themselves when they grow up and will be able to accomplish big things in the world. In contrast, God wants us to remind our children of who He is and who they are in Christ so they can grow up and become His ambassadors to the world.

The end game is not good behavior, but Christlikeness—and not merely for our teens. Before they can adjust their deeply held belief systems, they have to be able to see Christlikeness in us as well. We will continue to need to address bad behavior as well as brokenness in our children's lives, but before we dive into those deep waters, we have to be willing to pray for wisdom and change in our own lives if we are going to have influence in theirs.

Chapter 2

Seeing God's Design for Life

I was in my front yard talking to a friend on the phone when I overheard my neighbor talking to her pre-elementary son. She was expressing herself in a way we've all been guilty of as parents. With much frustration she complained, "Well, if you're not going to do it right, then let's just go inside and forget it." As I looked over, I saw her juggling a toddler on one hip while trying to teach her five year old how to ride his bike. Now, on most days, this single mom does a great job providing for her children, making sure their needs are met, and getting them where they need to be in order to give them a healthy childhood. But this particular day was a potential milestone day...and it was not going well. There was added pressure because it was the day of the First Bike Ride.

I quickly ended my phone call and offered to help. Since I had been through the first bike ride day with both of my own kids, I understood what a milestone it could be as well as the pressure that both parent and child could feel because of what was expected on this day. I asked what the problem seemed to be, and she answered, "Well, he won't listen to me." We have all been there, haven't we? But before jumping to conclusions, I took a look at the bicycle. I noticed the training wheels were on backwards and the handlebars were actually reversed. No wonder the child couldn't ride his bike!

Isn't this what happens to us many times? We cannot put the pieces together right in our own lives or in the lives of our children, yet we expect them to be able to function appropriately and on demand. We forget there is a process in everything.

After I adjusted the training wheels and turned the handlebars around on the boy's bike, then we could get into a few basic bike riding lessons from a parent's perspective. I suggested that instead of letting her son jump on the bike and heading down the cul-de-sac, maybe she could start with him up on the sidewalk. While I held the two year old, I encouraged the mom to walk alongside her son stabilizing the back of his bike with her hand as he made his first attempts at pedaling. After six tries up and down the sidewalk, the mom reflected, "I just don't remember it being this difficult when I was a kid."

The five year old had to use his entire body to maneuver the bike—his hands, his feet, his eyes, and his ears all working together to make everything work. Once an adult has done it for years, it is very hard to remember how hard it was at first. However, there are too many necessary steps to shortchange the process. She would never get the chance to see her child flying down the street with the flag waving on the back if she did not take him through the process.

Too often we do the same thing with our children when it comes to their spiritual lives. I think many times we try to jump in too far down the line from where our children need to be spiritually, instead of starting back at the beginning where they are. We try to jump ahead to get them where we think they should be and then get quickly frustrated when we don't see the desired results. We draw conclusions such as:

> *"My teenager just doesn't care anything about church."*

> *"I can't get my son to sit still long enough to listen to me read a family devotion."*

> *"I try to talk with my daughter about God, but she just shrugs her shoulders."*

*"The only way my ten year old would read the Bible
is if I paid him."*

Most of the time the problem isn't as black and white as we make it when it comes to spiritual maturity. Just as you would not let your eight year old jump into the deep end of the pool without knowing how to swim, you cannot expect your teenager to get anything out of going to a youth group without first developing a spiritual foundation.

If there are one hundred steps to achieving spiritual maturity, think of laying the right spiritual foundation as the first fifty steps. It is not something you do when your child is five and then automatically move to "deeper truths." The right spiritual foundation is something you start when your child is young and then revisit and reinforce every day.

I was watching an episode of *This Old House* on PBS. Yes, I am a proud PBS supporter and DIY nerd. The team was doing renovations on a beautiful Massachusetts home from the 1880s. The complete project would cost more than $500,000. As they began to tear into layer after layer of the subfloor and basement walls, they realized there was significant damage to the foundation. There weren't simply cracks; there were areas where the foundation was completely missing. The house was straining just to hold itself up. Before all of the ceramic tile floors, ornate wall molding, and handmade cabinets could go in, they had to take a week to tend to the foundation. There were also several different techniques to be used on the same foundation. It was no "one size fits all" solution.

I was struck by the detail spent on fixing a part of the house that no one would ever see. No one would ever question whether or not it was secure. The facade would always give the appearance that everything was okay. Yet, here was a home that more than a hundred years after it was built still required work on its foundation.

The spiritual foundation of your child's life is not something you lay and then move on to other more important matters of life. The truths you pour into them must be revised time and again. You are not merely laying a foundation in your child's life. You are starting the framework of the spiritual legacy for your family that will need to last for years to come.

Marking the Boundaries

The first step in laying a spiritual foundation in the life of your child is by marking the boundaries. Think back to when your child was a pre-toddler still putting things in his mouth and scooting or crawling around the house before he could do much of anything else. The day finally came when he started to pull himself up in preparation for trying to walk. As a proactive parent, you probably covered the outlets and removed breakable objects in anticipation of your child's newly developing abilities. You put latches on the lower cabinets and covers on the corners of the coffee table to make sure he would not hurt himself or others in the process. You cleared a path on the floor to ensure a successful experience as your child tried to do what he had seen you do thousands of times. You marked the boundaries so he knew where to go.

Your toddler doesn't yet understand the difference between spiritual bondage and freedom or how quickly happiness can turn to despair. He doesn't understand how our daily choices can lead us closer or farther away from the freedom we are meant to have in Christ. He has mastered pooping and eating—and that is about it.

Somewhere around three or four years of age, a child starts to see that basic choices can have consequences. Sticking his finger in certain places can hurt, or touching certain things in the kitchen can burn. This is also the time when he starts to learn about truth, responsibility, and proper ways to play with others. However, he cannot learn these principles on his own. He needs you to help him understand not only why truth is important, but also Who is the Author of truth. He needs you to show him how to be a friend to others, as well as to discover the One who is a friend to sinners.

One of my friends says it like this: "Until your child is old enough to know God, you will represent God to them." The reality is that for a time, you are the primary authority in your child's life. Before they know how to look to God for answers, they look to you. Before they can go to God for guidance, comfort, or nourishment, they go to you. In fact, in the formative years, all of a child's needs are met by his parents. While they are little, we begin to model for them what it means to live life. We can model dependency on God for better or for worse. We model humility and brokenness. We model strength and dignity.

As a child moves into early childhood and adolescence, parents are laying a foundation for the overarching idea of helping their child discover God and His design for life. Teaching God's overall design is key—not simply imparting a list of rules. Our job is not to be the rule-referee merely telling our children what they can and cannot do, but rather it is to model God's design for healthy relationships under authority. We all find ourselves saying, "Yes, No, Not now, Don't do this, Don't touch that, No you can't, Don't ask me again...." However, if you find yourself constantly repeating a moral cliché rather than instructing your children to find God's design, you may find that you are raising a good person rather than a redeemed believer. In the end, being a good, ethical person will do them no good for eternity. The ultimate goal must be deeper than growing up to be a morally sound citizen; the goal is for your child to become a transformed child of God.

Part of recognizing the process and marking the boundaries during adolescence is helping your child recognize God's design for life. The entire foundation of your relationship with your child and the reason God has entrusted them into your care is so you can help your child discover God's plan for life in general and for your child's life in particular. While there are 1,001 things we could talk about doing as parents—teaching skills, setting expectations, giving responsibilities—the most important thing you will ever do in the big scheme of things is to help your children discover who God is.

The Beauty of God's Design

When we go back to the beginning in Genesis, we can see how God was laying a foundation with man. That foundation would provide a way for man's heart to connect with God's heart. If you look at God as the ultimate parent with Adam and Eve, He gives direction for how to parent our own children. In Genesis 2:15-17, take a look at a passage that might shape how you lay that same foundation in the life of your own child.

> *"The Lord God took the man and put him in the Garden of Eden to work it and take care of it. And the Lord God commanded the man, 'You are free to eat from any tree in the garden, but you must not eat from the tree of the knowledge of good and evil, for when you eat from it you will certainly die."*

God's Design Gives Responsibility

The first thing you notice in God's design for mankind was that God gave responsibilities to man *"to work (in the Garden) and take care of it."* Part of helping our children to discover God's design for themselves is by giving them responsibilities. We can and should give them roles in our household at age-appropriate levels. It's good for a parent to entrust part of the task of keeping up the home to children—tidying a bedroom, taking out the trash, or caring for the dog. However, the task is not the end goal.

When God gave responsibilities to man, he was setting man apart from the rest of creation. In fact, mankind is the only part of creation to which God gives responsibilities. Perhaps the reason is that mankind is the only being to whom God also gives a conscience. Mankind is the only one uniquely designed to be able to look at something and deem its value. Mankind can evaluate art. Mankind can appreciate beauty. We can identify redeeming value, discern situations where a conscious choice is necessary, or determine whether or not an activity is going to be beneficial in our relationship with God or with other people. Because we are made in the image of God, He also entrusted us with those abilities.

God's design for life was to give mankind dignity, and He did that by giving us responsibilities. Likewise, we dignify our children by giving them responsibilities. It is not simply that I am tired of washing my child's clothes, so they have to do it. I am showing that I trust him to take responsibility for this part of our family. When our kids were little, the boundary marker we set up for our children was their bedroom. The room was theirs to keep in good condition by not damaging its walls or furniture, but also as a place to keep their possessions and clothing safe. It did not have to be meticulously kept straight at all times, but the toys had to be picked up before a friend could come over or when friends left. In contrast, our family room was a different matter. That space was to be shared by all of us in community, so at the end of each day, any belongings were to be removed from there and taken to a bedroom. If a child left toys or shoes in our shared space, it had the potential to inhibit our community (e.g., Mommy does not like smelling sweaty socks or stepping on Lego blocks).

Our son had the hardest time with this when he was six or seven years old. Our routine at night was to get ready for bed, talk for a bit, say prayers, and read a story. Many nights I would return to his room with a couple pairs of shoes, an armload of toys, or other miscellaneous items that I would tuck into the bed with him for the night. One night, he moaned in an exasperated tone, "Dad, why do you do this every night?" I responded, "Because you left your stuff in our family room. Now Mom and I can't enjoy our time together without getting Legos stuck in our toes and trying to avoid your smelly shoes." It wasn't about enforcing a rule that his stuff had to be put away; it was about working together within our home. We were trying to help him understand God's design for living in community and how we take care of one another. God gives us responsibilities, so we give our children responsibilities.

God's Design Provides Direction

The second thing God does in the garden is to provide direction for our lives. Notice the next sentence of the passage, "*And the Lord God commanded the man* [or directed the man]..." Here God gives direction by clearly communicating with Adam what is expected from him. Likewise, we get to do the same thing with our children. We give direction to their lives through what we communicate and how we instruct them.

I doubt it would have been fair for God to give this direction and freedom if man had already disobeyed God's design. If the man had already chosen to live outside of God's design without knowing God's direction beforehand, then things would have been unclear. Let's imagine that God had never told the man and woman what the boundaries were for life in the garden. It is only after having given His direction and boundaries to the man, and the man and woman consequently disobeying, that God comes looking for them in the garden to hold them accountable for their choice. God had clearly communicated the boundaries, but they had chosen to breach the boundaries. We do the same thing for our children.

On several occasions I have had to counsel parents whose children had gone off the rails. Their child's behavior and choices were causing not only serious distrust from their parents, but were ripping at the harmony of the entire family. Even if you haven't experienced a situation where your child's choices have life-changing consequences, I am sure you can relate to being disappointed in a significant choice your child has made.

As these parents would sit across from me and recall the choices of their child, I could see the simultaneous heartache and frustration. "Why in the world would she do this," or "Why would he go there?" were common responses. At some point, I would ask "Had you ever addressed this type of situation with your son or daughter?" The usual answer was, "No, but how could they not know it was wrong?"

I am sure their child knew the choice was going to be a bad idea. However, that still doesn't absolve mom and dad for not clearly communicating their expectations. Now, I am not talking about giving your teenager a laundry list of things they cannot do. That would be impossible. It is far more important that you set a bar for them by telling your child what your standards are for right living and right relationships in general.

When each of my teenagers got their first cell phones, they had to sign a cell phone contract with their mother and me that outlined our expectations for how they were to use their phone. When my son got his driver's license, we had a talk about the kind of driver I expected him to be. When my daughter started talking about how attractive boys are, you had better believe we had another conversation about our expectations and boundaries when it comes to relationships and dating.

God's Design Offers Freedom

A significant thing we can see in this passage is that God's design for life involves freedom. The passage says they were *"free to eat from any tree in the garden"* but not from the tree of good and evil. When I teach on this text at youth conferences, I ask the teenagers what part of the overall passage stands out to them as God's direction for their life. They almost always tell me that God's direction is "don't eat of a certain tree." They perceive that God's direction is about a rule or limitation. They think that from the very beginning God said, "Don't." But God's first direction was about setting them free. They were free to eat from any other tree in the garden.

We were designed for freedom. We were made to be creatures of freedom. God did not originally design us to be confined like a dog on a 10-foot chain. He did not say the delectable fruits of the garden were off limits. He did not intend for them to spend a miserable existence roaming from tree to tree, never getting to partake of any of the fruits they found. From the very beginning, God's plan for the man and woman was to be free to enjoy the beautiful place God had made with all of its delights.

In John 10:10, Jesus compares the enemy's intentions for us with his own. He says, *"The thief comes only to steal and kill and destroy; I have come that they may have life, and have it to the full."* A full life. Abundant life. Jesus is saying that He came so we could finally understand what the human experience was always supposed to be about since the beginning. Since the fall of man, humanity lived only in brokenness and sin, not knowing what a right relationship with God could be like. With His birth, Jesus made it possible for all of us to fully understand the life we were made for. He came to restore our freedom that had been missing because of sin. We could now be free from the remorse and shame of our actions, free from second-guessing, free from the destruction of relationships, free from the loss of our identity, and free from the hopelessness of our future. Hebrews 12:1 tells us we can throw off the sin that so easily entangles us.

Unfortunately, allowing freedom is probably one of the most difficult principles to apply in parenting. Since we are so intimately familiar with our own fallen condition, it seems to make sense to restrict freedom until it can somehow be earned. If you prove yourself trustworthy, then I can let you have the privilege you have been working for. Freedom is the unattainable carrot at the end of a stick. Since we have only lived in sin and brokenness, we can never truly hope to earn a place of freedom. But Jesus insists that he came to give life to the fullest, not to give life with restriction. We will ultimately get to experience freedom if we are able to recognize how to live fully within the boundaries of God's design.

God's Design Ensures Our Protection

From the beginning God made us to be free, but our freedom has always been connected to His protection. The two go together and cannot be separated. The reverse of God's principle is that if He is no longer protecting us, then we can have no hope for freedom.

Likewise, if we choose to be out from under His protection, we can no longer enjoy true freedom. If we are in a state of spiritual freedom, it is because we are under the umbrella of God's protection and authority. If in our freedom, we willingly submit to God's authority, then we can count on His protection.

God intended for mankind to enjoy freedom in the garden. At the same time, He knew that one tree would mean death as a consequence for eating it. He warned the man and woman how to remain freely within the boundaries of His protection by saying, *"When you eat of the tree...you will certainly die."* They had the freedom to choose. They knew His design. They enjoyed the freedom as well as God's protection.

Your child gets to experience the same principle of freedom in their relationship with you. All of the kitchen cleaners in your home come with a warning label in bold letters that say something along the lines of "Danger. Do Not Drink or Get in Eyes!" You know your favorite degreaser or *Goo-B-Gone* can cause harm, but when used responsibly everything is fine. I am guessing that before your children began to walk, you put latches on the cabinet where you stored your cleaners or put them on a tall shelf out of reach of grabbing hands and curious eyes. Keeping the squirt bottle out of sight wasn't a punishment. It was to ensure your precious one's protection and continued freedom not to have to visit a poison control center, have their stomach pumped at an emergency room, or have to drink ipecac.

We grieve when our children insist on going outside the boundaries of our protection by touching the hot stove thereby burning themselves and experiencing the loss of the freedom to enjoy a pain-free day. We see the betrayal they feel towards us for letting them get hurt. We hear the blame they place on us for not protecting them. They don't understand how the boundaries work, and they do not know that stepping outside the boundaries will mean a loss of freedom.

As children get older, their choices become more difficult and can carry real-world consequences. When they were young, you showed them God's design for how life and relationships work, but there comes a day when you no longer control their actions. I'm sure you can remember a time from your own experience growing up when you knew you were making a choice clearly outside of God's boundaries. Lying to your parent, taking advantage of a friend, cheating on a test—whatever the offense—at some point you had to deal with the wave of regrets and remorse.

I remember being a freshman in high school and all of the excitement and fear that came with starting school at a new campus. One of my favorite classes was an elective business class. It was the only "fun" class in my schedule, so I looked forward to it each day. I especially liked my teacher. She was engaging, passionate about teaching, and made me feel equal to some of the upperclassmen in the room. The more affirmation I got from her, the more I wanted to do well in the class.

Another strong personality in the class was a junior guy that sat to my left. He was popular, wore a letterman jacket, knew how to talk to girls, and wore just the right amount of cologne. He was basically everything I thought I needed to be but was not.

I typically made A's in the class and didn't stress over the tests. About halfway through the semester, we had one of our big unit tests and I knew I had aced it. The next day when we got our tests back, mine had a big fat red "0" in the top corner with a note from my teacher that simply read, "See me after class."

My teacher wasn't shocked that I only missed two questions on the test. But she was shocked that Mr. Popular missed the same exact two questions. Mr. Popular that sat *right next to me.* The jig was up. She knew we had cheated.

I was mortified. I was embarrassed. I could not look my teacher in the eyes because I felt such shame. I didn't care that Mr. Popular might somehow blame me for the whole thing. I didn't care that I might be the topic of hallway gossip for fifteen minutes. I didn't even care about my grade in the class. All I cared about was that this teacher, who I deeply respected, did not look at me the same way anymore. The look on her face said, "I can't trust you."

When we choose to live within God's boundaries, regardless of the pressure we feel from others, it is only then we experience the benefits of God's protection. So many "opportunities" the world throws at us sound good, but turn out to be a distortion of the freedom that God's design for life ensures. Consider our sexual choices. Let's get even closer to home—consider your teen's sexual choices. Our culture asserts that you are free to express your sexuality however you feel: Sex between two consenting adults is fun. If you want to look at porn, it doesn't really hurt anyone. If you truly love one another, sex is a good thing. If two girls (or two guys) want to be sexually intimate, it is their choice.

In working with teenagers for more than two decades, I cannot recall one time that a high school guy walked into youth group to announce, "Attention everyone. I just had sex with my girlfriend and it was the most incredible experience! It was everything I dreamed sex would be." On the contrary, I can remember many times both guys and girls coming to me in confidence as they struggled with feelings of regret, shame, and remorse from making a sexual choice that was outside of God's boundaries. Regardless if the issue is sexual intimacy, home relationships, school responsibilities, or work life, we experience God's protection and freedom only when we live within His design.

Seeing the Whole Picture

The same principle holds true when parenting teens. We communicate the boundaries. We provide protection. We enable them to enjoy freedom within the boundaries. Sometimes this means we talk about what the freedoms are before they can ever be lost. Within God's boundaries, a child will never feel regret. A tween will not have to deal with remorse. A teenager will avoid shame. There will be freedom from grief. There will be no reason to struggle with disbelief or doubt. In general, it is when we venture outside God's design that we begin to doubt God's protection. When we embrace unhealthy relationships, we face limitations to our freedom. When we look at things that are outside of God's boundaries, hide activities that are outside of God's boundaries, or excuse our participation in relationships outside of God's boundaries, we lose the benefits of His protection.

It falls to us as parents to explain to our children why God's design works better than trying to live life outside of His boundaries. We get to help our teens understand what God has made them to be as men or women of God. Before a child or teen has started a relationship with Christ, we are limited as to how much we can expect them to embrace. Each one is in process, and these principles primarily apply to those who want to know God's plan and are willing to explore what life might be like within His protection. Before that, we are limited to laying the groundwork, then waiting for the Holy Spirit to bring them to the place where they are ready to know God. When they recognize a need for Christ in their lives, then we can communicate the principles more personally.

If parents were honest, we would admit that many times our frustrations with our children's choices are because we expect them to be at our level of moral maturity. When it comes to understanding right and wrong or discerning what is acceptable versus off-limits, our children simply have not lived long enough to make sound judgment calls consistently. Whether your child is two or twenty-two, consider the following questions: *Can you trust that the Holy Spirit is doing His job of revealing truth, love, and purpose to your child? Can you trust that God's timing may be different from your own? Even if your child may go through some difficult failures, can you trust that the Creator, the One who knows them better than you do, is still at work, wooing them to Himself? Do you believe His way is better than your own?* These are tough questions, but important ones to grapple with.

We have all experienced the frustration of something breaking in our house. You're cruising along through life on all cylinders.

Everything is going great, then out of nowhere, the dishwasher breaks, the A/C goes out, or the kitchen cabinet falls off the wall. If you are like me, your first thought is, "I bet I can fix that," said with as much smug confidence as you can muster. After hours or days of endless frustration and futility, you think, "Well, at least I think I can rig it so that it will be usable."

My father-in-law was the king of rigging anything and everything. He had extra fishing line wrapped around every belt because "you just never know when you'll need it." I don't think he owned anything that did not have a piece of duct tape or scrap piece of rope tied to it. One day I was in his car and noticed a piece of rope looped in and out of his A/C vent. I asked its purpose and he responded, "It has been there so long, I don't even remember."

Isn't this how we parent at times? We get frustrated and impatient with God's timing and slow progress in our children's lives so we decide, "I can fix it." Or at the very least, I can rig it. We forget that the goal isn't merely obedient children. It's not simply to have a good kid. It is Christlikeness. It is to help them discover God's best for their lives. And that takes a lifetime of following Christ to grow into.

TRANSPARENCY EXERCISE

Over the next week, as you address behavior issues with your children, begin to look for an opportunity to share about a time when you made a choice outside of God's boundary as a child or teenager. It could be the time you stole something from a friend, got caught lying, received your first speeding ticket, etc. As you share your story, explain God's design in the situation and how your decision limited your freedom. Explain what the consequences were for you. Perhaps you didn't get into trouble for a long time and had to struggle with the issue. How did the choice change your relationship with someone else? End the conversation by reassuring your child that the reason you share these stories is because you understand how hard it is to choose God's best in life and because you understand the pressures they will be facing as well.

Chapter 3

Walking Together in God's Design

Recently our son was having a moment of panic and dread because he didn't know what colleges to apply to. He has good grades and he does well on standardized tests, but he doesn't have a specific direction for a major or focus of study. To him, the "what ifs" are brutal. *What if I can't figure out what school to go to? What if I don't make it when I get there? What if things don't work out and I have to do something else altogether?* At times like this, I know it is my job to help him put the brakes on and reflect on what he knows to be true. *Who does God say you are? Ultimately, who is responsible for directing your path? What does God say about how much you are worth to Him? What does He promise about the future plans He has for you?* The rule of thumb in our culture has always been, "Get a diploma, get a degree, and get a good job." However, when these rules fail, it is my job to remind him about God's design for his life. There is freedom and protection in that.

Taking the conversations back to God's design requires that we resist merely repeating a set of rules. When you boil every situation down to a moral absolute or insist, "You can do this" or "You can't do that," it cheapens God's design. Instead, enter into the conversation with your teen by respecting the boundaries, recognizing the freedom, and appreciating the protection inherent in living according to God's design.

When your child does something wrong that you have to correct and they question "why," analyze whether you have said one of the following (while admitting the side thoughts):

- ☑ "I just need you to do this for me." (Because it's all about me as a parent being happy.)
- ☑ "I don't have time to explain." (Just enough time to demand.)
- ☑ "You obey me, then we'll talk about it." (Although I probably won't get around to that.)
- ☑ "Don't argue with me." (As if asking a question is disrespectful.)
- ☑ ...and the dreaded "Because I said so." (I swore I would never go there.)

I have been guilty of every one of these. How about you? Life gets busy and we look for shortcuts. It's much quicker to bark out Do's and Don'ts than to have a conversation. Unfortunately, your commands do not transform your child's heart. A change of heart happens when you are willing to have the long talks and to meet with your teen in a loving relationship and teachable moment.

In the gospels, we see Jesus repeatedly using this pattern of teaching. When the woman caught in adultery is brought before Jesus, He asks her the question, "Who is it here that condemns you?" "No one," she responds. Jesus extends grace telling her that He doesn't condemn her either. It's only after establishing her forgiveness that He gives the command, "Now go and sin no more."

Remember the similar pattern when Jesus talked with Peter after his betrayal. Jesus repeatedly asked Peter, "Do you love me?" After each "yes" from Peter, Jesus stated the command, "Feed my sheep." Whether Jesus was fishing with His disciples, having dinner with a crooked tax collector, or talking about heaven with a Pharisee, Jesus' commands always came in the context of a relationship and teachable moment.

In the last chapter, we investigated God's design for life and the principles necessary for the kind of life that God made us. Now we need to unpack it bit further to see what that looks like in everyday living with your teen. If issuing blanket statements for the kind of behavior we want is a shortcut (and ineffective), then what do we do about situations or behavior that arise every day and catch us unprepared? The key is taking the time to explain and walk in God's design together.

The hard (and uncomfortable) conversations Mona and I find ourselves having with our children, all revolve around moral boundaries and living Christlikeness. When they were younger, we spent countless hours talking about honesty, personal responsibility, being a good friend, and the importance of generosity. I remember being worn out from some of the talks with our independent-thinking daughter. She would ask "why" to every request or simply not do it until personally convinced of the benefit. Now that she is older, we look back on those conversations as almost simple compared to the weightiness of the talks we are having in the teen years.

As a former youth pastor, I have experienced countless conversations with teenagers about love, sex, dating, pornography, etc. I can tell you, it's completely different having those conversations with my own son and daughter. I feel like I should seek out and apologize to every parent that I flippantly gave counsel to as a young pastor by saying, "Suck it up and have 'The Talk' with your kid." When I had to live out those conversations first-hand with my own teenagers, I admit they were not as easy as I thought they would be. I didn't enjoy having to sit with my son and talk about how to respond to the temptations of digital porn or telling my daughter what to do if a boy makes her physically uncomfortable. Yet, I still broached the subjects, because if I did not, no one else would. Your child is looking for you to stand in the gap for them as well. They need you to be the one to have those talks that equip them with life skills and street smarts. In a moment of uncertainty, you will be glad you did.

Answering the Why Questions of Everyday Life

Your children will encounter moral choices every day of their lives. From pressures to cheat at school to temptations to compromise integrity on a date, these situations are inescapable. As you work through specific situations with your children, it is important that you continue to clarify God's boundaries. For example, we would all agree that within God's design for life, lying is not an acceptable behavior. But why is lying wrong? Consider the different responses we typically give our children when it comes to lying.

"God wants you to be good and good people do not lie." In this scenario what God (and you as a parent) is most concerned about is goodness. What you end up teaching your child to be is a moralist. Moral goodness is the highest value.

"The more dishonest you are with me, the less I can trust you." We have all used this one, too. You tell the truth because things work out better for you if you do. You will get farther in life with other people if you are trustworthy. While each of these statements are true, if you don't go deeper, what you end up teaching your child to be is a pragmatist.

"I am not happy with you. You need to go think about what you have done." Besides being emotionally manipulative, this teaches your child that what is most important is happiness, particularly the parent's happiness. Your child learns that their good behavior leads to happiness—and that they are responsible for making everyone happy. This is at the heart of humanism not the heart of God.

All of these statements are *partly* true, but they also fall short of painting a whole picture of God's design for us. None of them answer the question of why God tells us not to lie. The issue is much bigger than mere goodness, happiness, or practical relationships.

Everything that God permits or prohibits is because of His character. This is the key to helping your child understand godly behavior. We are made in the image of our Creator and who we are should be a reflection of His image—His character.

My 14-year-old daughter was sitting in the hammock next to me, when out of nowhere she said, "Dad, in class today we were talking about the creation story. I know God said, 'It was very good' when He made man, but why does it even matter that we are made in God's image?" I'm grateful that my daughter is grappling with such a difficult question because it illustrates a profound truth that resides at the heart of how we should parent.

Being made in the image of God is what makes us unique among all of His creation. We are the only beings in creation that have a conscience that can know good from evil. We can look at a painting and determine if it is beauty or debauchery. We can feel how we are treated by another and know if it is love or hatred. But it is not merely that we can know goodness, determine beauty, and feel love. The kicker is that we are called to be bearers of these things.

The apostle Paul says as much in 1 Peter 1:14-16 when he tells us, *"As obedient children, do not conform to the evil desires you had when you lived in ignorance. But just as he who called you is holy, so be holy in all you do; for it is written: 'Be holy, because I am holy.'"*

The ubiquitous WWJD wristbands so popular in the '90s may have caused people to question their actions, but in general they missed the mark. The question cannot always be, *"What would Jesus do?"* Many of the situations our teens face today are not even addressed in the gospels. I can't say with certainty if Jesus would play video games, listen to secular music, or connect with strangers on social media. Instead of grappling with the unknown, the question we have to help our children answer is, *Who is this Jesus that loves me?* All the issues you will help your child navigate in life come back to knowing how Jesus loves us.

The more time you spend helping your child connect with Jesus and understand what it means to walk in a right relationship with him, the more behavioral issues tend to take care of themselves. This doesn't mean your child will never make foolish or unwise choices at times, but by and large, the more rooted they are in Christ, the more likely they are to have consistency in their life path.

His love for us and our love for Him is exactly where Jesus places the emphasis when He was laying the foundation of His kingdom on earth. Consider the following statements from or about Jesus:

"As the Father has loved me, so have I loved you. Now remain in my love."

— John 15:9

"We love because he first loved us."

— 1 John 4:19

"If you love me, you will keep my commands."

— John 14:15

"Whoever has my commands and keeps them is the one who loves me."

— John 14:21

"Love each other deeply, because love covers over a multitude of sins."

— 1 Peter 4:8

There is an order to our lives that begins with the Father's love. The Father loves Jesus; in turn Jesus loves us. The only reason we can love is because we have been loved. If we love Jesus, we will end up obeying Him. Obedience is the evidence of our love. Finally, it is our love for one another that begins to restore our relationships.

A fascinating turn of events occurs when Jesus spends the evening in the home of a shady tax collector named Zacchaeus. When confronted with the love and truth of who Jesus is, a transformation begins in Zacchaeus' life, which causes him to return all he had stolen from others. The part we miss is that Jesus didn't tell him to return the money. It was an internal work of the Holy Spirit in Zacchaeus' heart that caused him to stop doing evil and show the love of Christ to others. God's grace led to Zacchaeus' goodness.

Likewise, your child is far more willing to obey you if they know you love them and have their best interest at heart. Often when I have one of those uncomfortable conversations about something one of my children has done wrong, I start the conversation by asking, "Do you believe I love you?" and "Do you believe I have your best interest at heart?" Even when they know a confrontation is coming, If they can affirm those truths, I know they will be willing to receive instruction from me.

Something Has Got to Change

Don't misunderstand. I am not saying that loving your children means you do not need to worry about correcting their behavior. On the contrary. Face correction head on, but from a posture of helping them understand who God made them to be. This requires you to always have the end game in sight.

When a football coach makes a game plan, he has more than one hundred plays from which to choose. His players have memorized every one of those plays. They have run them endlessly in practices. They even plan for contingencies in case a play falls apart. Properly executing the plays is another step that gets the team closer to achieving the coach's end game. The coach's end game is not to score a touchdown, to have the fastest receivers, or to provide the best highlight reel for *Sports Center*. The end game is consistent— to win the game.

I read a biography on Bobby Fisher, whom many consider the greatest chess player of all time. His game play was a frequent topic of conversation. At chess exhibitions he could be seen playing ten games at once. When questioned how he was able to simultaneously beat so many opponents, he described his ability to look ahead to the big picture. Within a couple of moves of each game, he was able to both read his opponent *and* discern what was required in order to win. Every move he made was with the end game in mind.

When it comes to addressing your child's behavior, you have an end game as well. Your words and actions speak volumes to your child about what is most important to you in any situation. Your end game is one of three ideas:

CHANGING MY CHILD'S FEELINGS	CHANGING MY CHILD'S BEHAVIOR	CHANGING MY CHILD'S HEART

Before we start peeking behind the curtains to see which one of these you embrace, let's go ahead and admit two things together. One, we have all done all three of these. Two, ultimately we cannot change any of these situations. The more you believe you can change your child's feelings, behavior, or heart, the more frustrated, tired, and beat up you will feel as a parent. Ultimately, it has to be the work of God to change your child. Nonetheless, each of us plugs away at how we can "fix" things.

Changing My Child's Feelings

You know that Facebook manipulates you every time you get on the site or app. And you love it. Seriously, you do. It's why you keep coming back. Facebook used a team of data scientists (whatever that is) to find out why we keep coming back to the site over and over. Their research found that if you see too many posts in your feed from friends who talk about how great their lives are, you will start to feel that your own life doesn't compare and you will come back less often. Likewise, if you see too many posts from friends who share frustrations or things wrong with life, you will start feeling agitated and come back less often.

When you log onto your page and click "Top Stories," what you are actually seeing is a balance of just the right stories from friends that Facebook wants you to see in order to keep you emotionally buoyant. You never truly see what is happening in all of your friends' lives because Facebook manipulates your reality and in turn manipulates your emotions. You feel happy, just where they want you to be.

Sadly, emotional manipulation is a common ritual with parents as well. We wrongly learned long ago that relationships work best when we get our way. Whether it was a boyfriend/girlfriend or a parent, if we whipped out the tears we could get our way. For some of us, yelling or screaming worked to get someone else to cave. Other times we used words like a twisting knife to get others to agree with us or change their minds. Now we have functioned that way so long, we don't even recognize when it is happening.

We have all been guilty of expressing, "I cannot believe you just did that...again" or "How many times have we gone over this?" or "Are you just trying to make me mad?" These comments can become easy tools to get your child to feel guilty or manipulate their emotions. Keeping track of failures or reminding someone of how many times they have sinned usually results in giving them only enough motivation to get better at hiding their actions so they don't continue to get caught. However, they never grasp why the action was not appropriate for achieving the goal they originally meant to attain.

Emotions are a significant part of our makeup as creatures made in the image of our Creator. Depending on the moment, an emotion of sadness, joy, remorse, anger, or frustration might be an appropriate response. The difficulty is making sure that you aren't pulling a Facebook fast one and manipulating the emotional response to fit what you think needs to happen. Manipulation does not change hearts. Conviction does. Conviction is from the Holy Spirit; not from you or me.

Before walking into the next tense conversation with your child, stop and pray for three things.

- **Pray for clarity of truth in the conversation.** Ask God to help you speak plainly without emotions that can sabotage the teachable moment. Ask God to help you to stick to the topic at hand and not bring your own baggage or your child's past mistakes into the equation unless there is an acknowledged pattern of disrespect/disobedience concerning this issue.

- **Pray for conviction of sin from the Holy Spirit**. Speak the truth, and then allow the Holy Spirit to do His job of bringing conviction that leads to a change in heart. It may take time. Be willing to step back and wait.

- **Pray for the ability to speak with a balance of authority and understanding**. Your child needs to see that you have the authority and life-experience to understand what is happening and why. Your authority allows you to give boundaries, but your life-experience will help you extend grace.

Changing My Child's Behavior

Changing behavior is where much of our parenting takes place. We just want our children to stop doing things that make us want to beat our heads against a wall. Your five year old will not stop throwing things, your ten year old keeps picking on his sister, and your sixteen year old is unable to talk with you without rolling her eyes. Mom wants the chores done without whining and Dad wants the kids to stop yelling at each other. If we can just make the bad behavior stop, then everything would be okay.

We will go to almost any length to get our way as a parent. We end up saying and doing things that would make it onto the list of "Top Ten Things to Never Do As a Parent." We yell. We cry. We manipulate. We spank. We give timeouts. We take away cell phones, toys, privileges, etc. It makes us exhausted and our children resentful.

There are a number of YouTube videos of parents taking extreme measures in order to change their child's behavior. You've probably seen the one of the dad taking a shotgun to his daughter's laptop because he was angry about her attitude on social media. There is also the one of a dad that shredded his son's video games with his riding mower while his son is screaming in the background. Then there are the ones of the parent that microwaved his son's cell phone, the couple that reassembled their child's entire bedroom contents neatly in the backyard, and the mom that made her son wear a sandwich board while standing on the street corner, which announced to passersby, "I am wearing this because I lied to my Momma."

When we hear of those stories, a part of us wants to proclaim with a hand held high, "YES! You go, Dad! Rock on, Mom!" I have seriously contemplated burning the Xbox, selling my teenager's phones on eBay, and enjoying a nice vacation with the proceeds. Yes, I have! But in the end game, what would it accomplish?

Regardless of the poor behavior your child may be displaying, when you respond with actions that produce bitterness, rage, extreme shame, or empty coldness within your child, then you are not leading them to a godly response. You must keep the end game in mind and continue to ask what you want to see changed in your child. The objective is not to win the "battle of wills" between you and your child. The goal is a transformed heart into the image of Christ.

Your child is more shrewd than you may give them credit for. They learn very quickly what pleases you and what sets you off; what opens your heart toward them and what shuts you down. If obedience is what you value most, it doesn't take long for your child to figure it out. If they have hit the double digits in age, then they know how to play your game, especially if your game is "Be a good boy."

Scripture is clear that it is a parent's responsibility to discipline children, and what the results will be if we do not. Scripture also gives a specific purpose for godly discipline and oddly enough, it's not to produce obedience. Instead, discipline is intended to create a wealth of wisdom in our child.

Proverbs 29:15 says, *"Wise discipline imparts wisdom; spoiled adolescents embarrass their parents"* (The Message). Two principles are clearly seen here. One, we must address poor behavior in our children lest it lead to a spoiled heart. Two, the way we discipline should impart wisdom. Here is the big question to continually ask yourself: *In the methods you use to discipline your child, do they leave the conversation knowing what not to get caught doing next time or do they leave feeling better equipped to honor God with their choices next time?* Depending on your answer, your child will either grow up learning to play the false obedience game or they will grow up to be a man or woman that lives in a right relationship with God and others.

Changing My Child's Heart

Right relationship—this is the golden ticket to obedience. True obedience is always rooted in a loving relationship. Jesus asks for complete obedience from us, but it is not a blind obedience. He doesn't ask for trust without the foundation of a relationship first.

In John 13-17, Jesus spends the last night before His betrayal with His closest disciples. The culmination of investing three years in the lives of these men comes down to this last night. Jesus talks to them about knowing His love and loving one another. He tells them that others will know God's love by the way they love and that love is expressed by how they live. He talks about staying rooted in Him as the true vine and then they will bear fruit. After talking at great length about the relationship they have developed together, Jesus utters the words, "If you love me, you will obey me." Notice that He didn't say, "Obey me and somewhere along the way you'll start to love me, and then you will understand my demands." Instead, the world was changed by a group of men (and women) who were so transformed by Christ's love that they were able to turn the world on its edge through the extent of their loving obedience.

Jesus knew we only follow those whom we love. The same is true of your child. Your child can be compliant out of obligation. They can obey you with their actions, but resent you with their heart. I've been telling my own children since they were young that I care far more about us being in a right relationship with one another than I do about them being good. I know that if they love me, they will trust me. If they trust me, then they will obey me. You have to fight the urge to focus on simply correcting bad behavior, then lead the way Jesus did by building a right relationship between you and your child. This relationship of love is what leads to a changed heart.

A tragic part of Israel's history is the destruction of Jerusalem and the temple of God in 586 BC. Generation after generation of sin led to God allowing the tribe of Judah to be destroyed and taken into captivity by Babylon. Despite their abandonment of God's ways, He still sent hope through the message of the prophets. One such prophet, Ezekiel, told how they would be restored as a nation. It all came down to a change in their hearts.

> *"I will sprinkle clean water on you, and you will be clean; I will cleanse you from all your impurities and from all your idols.*
>
> *I will give you a new heart and put a new spirit in you; I will remove from you your heart of stone and give you a heart of flesh. And I will put my Spirit in you and move you to follow my decrees and be careful to keep my laws.*
>
> *Then you will live in the land I gave your ancestors; you will be my people, and I will be your God."*
>
> Ezekiel 36:25-28

Israel's redemption started with a work of God. He cleansed them of sin. He put His spirit in them, which enabled them to live a life of obedience to God's ways. When this happened, they were able to become the people God intended them to be all along. That, too, is how we are made right with God. If you and I have any hope of becoming the parents God intends for us to be, then we must allow Him to do the same work in us—to give us a new heart. We require a daily renewing of His spirit at work in us before we can ever set out to ask God to change our children's hearts.

Removing One Weed at a Time

I know what you're thinking now. "Okay, wait. It is starting to look like having all of these conversations is going to take an awful lot of time. I'm already busy enough just trying to get through one day into the next. I don't know if I can keep a conversation going beyond fixing it for the moment and moving on. I don't know that I can keep explaining the same thing over and over until my teenager gets it. It sounds exhausting." Yes, it is. However, it is worth it. The deepening relationship, personal maturity, and self-reliance you desire for your children as they get older doesn't happen by casual conversations now and then or by interjecting yourself into their lives when there is a problem. It happens by consistently taking small steps throughout their lives.

Ten years ago Mona and I were on a hike in the Ozark mountains. While under the cool shaded canopy of the tall oaks we looked down and saw the cutest blue flowers growing in clover-like clumps. We dug up a few thinking they would look good in our well-maintained flower garden. And they did for the first year. The next summer our beautiful lawn, shrubs, and organic garden were taken over with Wild Violets. I am convinced that these were one of the species that developed alongside thorns and mosquitos after the fall of man.

We spent the better part of the next year trying to find a way to combat our new nemesis. We tried boiling water, vinegar, and hot sauce. I even broke down and went with a chemical herbicide. Nothing could stop the growing blue carpet. I finally found one product I'm sure has been banned by the government for causing all kinds of cancers. It killed the plant and everything else within a square foot. Or so it seemed. Within weeks, the brown patches of dead grass showed a familiar small clover emerging from the ground to taunt me. In the end, there were only two ways to get rid of this monster weed. Option one was to dig a foot down, remove all of the sod in my lawn, and start over. It would be quick, like detonating a caustic bomb across the yard. Option two was to sit in the yard and dig them up one by one with a garden fork. Actually Mona came up with a third option. She said, "We could always just move and leave it to someone else." I went with option two.

Hours upon hours of tugging at the weed and its insidious root system is how I spent the next spring and summer. If I had fifteen minutes to spare, I would be outside pulling weeds. It took a maniacal determination. I'm sure I could look at the positive and say, "It was therapeutic." But in reality it was just tough, monotonous, mind-numbing work. I could also be tempted to say, "Everything is better now," but that would be a lie. Years later, from time to time, I still have to sit in my lawn and pull up the mistakes of my past. I think if I were to stop, one small errant weed could lead into a full-blown infestation again.

The same diligence required to invest in your child's spiritual and relational health will pay a lifetime of dividends that you cannot yet see. Focusing on a teen's heart doesn't usually bring about a quick change. It is a small seed of truth planted repeatedly over time. Your child doesn't need you to be an authority that flies in like a crop-duster trying to quickly fix things. They need for you to be willing to sit with them in their sin and brokenness, tug at the weeds together, and interject words of truth as the Lord leads you. Show them God's process in your own life so they can see that He is at work in them as well.

Setting the Right Bar

After you explain God's design for life to your children, you must be willing to live out His design alongside them. Honesty, integrity, compassion, service. We have the responsibility to model for our children what each of these qualities looks like in the big picture of the Christian life. At the same time, more less-favored qualities such as humility, peacemaking, repentance, and willingness to submit to authority are our responsibility to model as well. Your child watches and takes cues from you more than anyone else. For better or worse, they see how real or how relevant God is to life by watching you.

When you daily "take up your cross" and "offer yourself as a living sacrifice," God continues the transformation in your life to become like His son. The fruit of the spirit—love, joy, peace, patience, kindness, goodness, faithfulness, gentleness, and self-control—isn't something we strive for or try to do. It is a way of living that God does in us as we submit to Him. Just as you desire this for yourself, you must set the bar for your child that this is the life God designed them to have, too.

A mentor of mine used to say, "It is reasonable to expect those who profess to be followers of Christ to live by Christlike standards." Children who have not yet chosen to be followers of Christ might be willing to submit to their parents, but I don't expect them to obey out of a sense of being connected to God's heart or transformed by His Spirit in their lives. However, if your teen has professed Christ and you have communicated the principles of God's design, then you can begin to live out God's standards together. In other words, you set a bar for them as you live for Christ together.

So often, I encounter parents who are reeling from watching their teenagers spiral into sin that seems unconquerable. They have resigned themselves to the condition of brokenness and shame that they feel will be their new normal. For all of their good intentions, they cannot fathom how their child got into such a state to begin with. After a long process of helping the parent see their child's responsibility in the situation, I have to address the parent's role in how they got there. This is the question I ask: "Did you ever set a definitive bar for your child—paint a picture for them—of the life God meant for them to live?"

We live in a culture that seems afraid to set a bar of moral excellence. Compromising, justifying actions, and settling for mediocrity is rampant in the world we live in today. From the time my son was eight, I started having conversations with him about what it means to be a man. I've put him in contact with other men that live the Christian life the way I believe God means for it to be lived. I've told him stories of his grandfathers and their walks with the Lord. I've shared with him both failures and triumphs in my own life. All of this has been done to say to him, "Here is the bar. This is what it looks like to honor God as a man."

He has given his life to Christ, he has a great relationship with us, and he has wisely chosen his friends. Even with these he is still a teenage boy in process, which means that sometimes he blows it—big time. But when he does, the bar doesn't change. We walk together back into holiness and wholeness. I don't have the prerogative to lower the bar just because the choices he has to face get harder the older he gets.

During the 1992 U.S. Olympic trials, the sure bet for gold in the decathlon was Dan O'Brien. He had won the world championship the previous year and was dubbed the "World's Greatest Athlete." So sure was his win that Reebok and NBC Sports spent a fortune on Dan as the centerpiece of their advertising as Olympic sponsors.[1]

On the final day of the trials, Dan was in first place going into the eighth event—the pole vault. Attempting 5'9", Dan clipped the bar and had to try again. He failed a second time. Then a third time. On his last attempt, Dan once again failed to clear the height. As the bar came tumbling down, the sports world sat in shocked silence. The world's greatest athlete would not be going to the Olympics. It didn't matter that he was the reigning world champion. It didn't matter that he was in first place up until that moment. The only thing that mattered was he did not clear the bar.

Dan could have responded to his public embarrassment by saying, "At least I was great for a moment" or "All things considered, my past accomplishments should be good enough for me to qualify." Instead of fading into the category of "forgotten sports heroes," he was determined to come back. To do so, he couldn't lower the bar or expect any favors. Instead he set the bar even higher. Dan O'Brien went on to win the World Championship the next year in 1993 and again in 1995. His career was completed at the 1996 Olympics in Atlanta were he went on to win the gold metal.

When your child has a moral failure, whether willfully or unintentionally, you must respond by setting the bar for them. You don't change your expectations. You don't lower God's standard. The goal is always the person of Christ. And that goal is best accomplished when you run toward Christ together.

Giving Freedom Within God's Design

Perhaps the most difficult part for us in teaching our children God's design for life is being willing to give them freedom within His design. Allowing freedom doesn't mean you allow your child to have whatever they want or to choose something that is clearly outside of God's boundaries. Freedom within God's design is all about letting them become who God has made them to be. Again to be clear, I am talking about the freedom to make their own choices *within* God's design.

Let's say your child is living within God's design for his or her life. They are respectful to you. They are showing personal responsibility. They are making wise choices overall. They have healthy relationships with others. For all practical purposes, things are going well. Now let's consider a few different scenarios.

1. Your child is eight. She walks into the living room on Saturday night and says, "Can I wear this to church tomorrow?" In her hand she is holding her favorite red and white striped skirt, and yellow top, and a pair of purple Chuck Taylor high-top Converse sneakers.

2. Your child is in middle school. While riding in the car with you to school one morning, he blurts out, "Can I grow my hair long? You know, like those guys in rock bands?"

3. Your child is now in high school. One night at dinner she questions, "You guys know my boyfriend, Thomas? He's going on a college visit and he wants me to come with him for the weekend so just the two of us can spend time together. What do you think?"

Your immediate reaction may be to say "no" in every situation, but as we talked about at the beginning of the chapter, keep the end game in mind. You might think your eight year old will look ridiculous wearing her mismatched outfit, but what is she asking for? Simply for some self-expression within God's boundaries. You might not like the idea of living with a grunge rocker, but what is your son asking for? An opportunity to explore his identity within God's boundaries.

The third situation is drastically different. There are significant red flags. Something in you is screaming, "Danger! System overload! Possible explosion! Run!" Regardless of your daughter living personally within God's boundaries, this situation could possibly set her up for a moral failure. It's an unequivocal "no-go."

It's important that you choose your battles wisely. Just because your child wants to do something that you would not choose doesn't automatically make it wrong. Many times it comes down to personal preference. As your child grows, their interests, hobbies, and personal style are going to change faster than a middle schooler's weekly crush. My kids have done karate, horse riding, paintball, basketball, baseball, swing dancing, long hair, pink hair, etc. You get the picture. Because of their willingness to live within God's design—and His boundaries—I am able to take joy in letting my kids try things that I wouldn't necessarily do.

As much as possible, be a "yes" parent, by giving your tweens and teens the freedom to discover themselves within God's boundaries. Saying "no" in too many non-moral situations can cause your child to lose creativity, stop taking positive risks, quit trusting God, and stop listening to your own authority. As you walk in a healthy relationship together, it makes it easier for you to read the situation and know when to say yes, no, or delay the opportunity until a better time.

There will inevitably be situations that you cannot allow even though it is not necessarily forbidden by God's word. At times, the Holy Spirit will impress a particular standard upon your conscience that is not strictly mandated in Scripture. These are convictions for you or your family that you should feel free to follow. These could include things such as the types of movies you watch, when your child can date, who they can spend time with outside your home, etc.

When these situations arise, it is a good idea for you to explain to your child that you feel prompted by the Holy Spirit in the choice you are making. This will help your child to see that you are being led by the Lord in your parenting decisions and to learn to trust your judgment in gray areas. That does not mean your child (or especially teenager) will agree with your decision, but when they see the track record you have of being led by God in making decisions, they are more likely to respect your choice for them.

Not too long ago, I had to deny my son a privilege that he was looking forward to. I couldn't even tell him the details of why I had to limit his participation in a particular event because it would compromise the integrity of someone else involved. I never doubted his character or his personal maturity, but I felt strongly that Bailey did not need to go. I even grieved not being able to leave the decision up to him, as he could not know the details of the situation. Clearly the Holy Spirit was throwing up red flags and I needed to listen.

After much serious reflection, I simply had to say no without detailed explanation. I made him aware of my decision as delicately as I could. I felt the tension of trying to explain my struggle to make a wise choice on his behalf without betraying a confidence. Honestly, I was nervous that he would respond with bitterness or resentment. Instead my decision was met with grace and understanding.

He said, "Dad, I still want to go, and now I am dying to know what happened to make you so serious about this. But I know you have never misled me before, so I trust you. I don't have to go this time."

I was stunned. It wasn't the response I was prepared for. The phrase my mind kept coming back to was "You have never misled me before." The importance of those words were both terrifying and humbling at the same time. I was moved that he would place such weight on my judgment and saw the seriousness that my choices have in his life.

When our conversation ended, Bailey walked away still half disappointed, but in that moment I felt the Holy Spirit say, "This wasn't about you, Brian. This was about Me. It is a work that I have been doing in your relationship with your son. This happened because of a lifetime of choices together."

The same thing is happening right now with you and your children. As they watch you, as they walk with you, as they are led by you, God is knitting your hearts together. A bond of trust and respect is developing. It is a work that happens when you submit yourself to God and to His will for your family. Take joy in knowing that before He ever blessed you with your children, this relationship was part of His design for you.

Chapter 4

Teaching Balance One Step at a Time

My daughter has taken ballet lessons since she was four years old. A lot has changed over that time, but I can still remember her first recital. The girls ranged in age from four through eighteen. The wee little ones always had the largest groups in the recital. There is nothing more adorable in the world than 30 four-year-old girls dressed in black leotards, pink tights, and fuchsia skirts bounding across a stage. But to call it ballet would be a stretch.

Even after months of practice, precious few of the girls have the same rhythm at the same time. They all run in somewhat the same direction as they dance across the stage, but to say they are dancing is a little misleading. Some of them look like those plastic toys that you push on the bottom to make their arms and legs fly out. A few of them lose their balance and tumble Pete Rose style across the stage. One keeps tugging at a skirt that has fallen to her knees, and two of them are left behind after they stop to wave to their parents in the audience. There is nothing particularly artistic about the experience, yet it is still beautiful somehow. It is beautiful because this is what we expect from them at four years old. They are just beginning the process of what we know they can become.

All parents are proud and entertained by our little girls, but when the older girls take the stage everything changes. These young women, like my daughter ten years into it, have been honing their skills for years. With their pointe shoes on and arms raised as high as they can reach, there is a gentle gracefulness as they glide across the stage. It feels almost like a holy moment as they move in unison in perfect harmony with the music. After years of discipline, practice, and undivided attention to their instructor, the girls have achieved the delicate rhythm and balance that is required in ballet.

If you think back a few years, you can remember the time you taught your son or daughter to ride a bike. You didn't just plop your child down on the seat and say, "Now, take off." Even if your child had the physically intuitive body of an Olympic gymnast, he would never have learned to ride were it not for a little help from training wheels. Those additional wheels gave your child the self-confidence and assurance he needed to make it to the end of the sidewalk. They helped your child keep the bike pointed in the right direction and gave him the balance he needed when he could not have done it on his own. Two five-inch hard rubber wheels are what kept your child safe and ensured that he could enjoy learning to ride a bike. Without the aid of the training wheels, he might never have gotten the hang of the "big boy bike."

Our son started riding with training wheels at about three years old. I lost count of how many half-mile trips around our neighborhood we took together. One time he even had those little wheels smoking as we rode more than a mile around Patriot Lake in East Memphis. After more than a year, as his long legs grew, I extended the training wheels as far as they would go. Finally, I knew it was time for a change; a change that wouldn't be easy for him.

As we pulled our bikes into the garage after a ride one afternoon, I casually hinted at the next step by saying, "You're getting just about too big for your training wheels aren't you?"

He didn't bite. I gently pressed further. "How would you feel about trying it one time without the training wheels?"

With big frightful saucer eyes he pointedly said, "I don't want to ride without my training wheels."

The next month or so was a series of questions and promptings that were met with the same firm response one would give a person selling magazines at their front door. "No thank you. Don't need it. Not interested."

It didn't matter if I appealed to his boyhood desire to be like his dad, the fact that he could go so much faster without them, or his sense of manhood (whatever that means to a five year old), he would not budge about giving up his training wheels. What once was a necessary tool to teach balance had become a crutch keeping him from knowing freedom on a bike.

After months of bargaining and reassuring, Bailey reluctantly let me take off the training wheels. I placed one hand on his seat and the other on his handlebar and we slowly started moving down the street. As he peddled, it would have looked to a bystander as if he had never peddled a bike before. For all practical purposes, that was true since biking without training wheels was a completely new experience for him. It was both starting over and moving forward at the same time.

If we were to go back even further, you can remember your child's first big lesson in balance as they learned to pull up. After about six months of kicking, scooting, and pushing around on the floor, your little rug rat was ready to stand and walk. Most children don't magically pull themselves up by a chair arm and start marching across the floor. It starts with pulling themselves up...and then falling down. Over and over and over again. But the day finally comes when they don't fall over. They stand awkwardly on their own two feet having conquered their first obstacle toward mobility. They may have been able to stand on their own, but to get anywhere at this point would still require your help.

Stashed away on a VHS tape somewhere in a closet is the sequence that happened next. Standing was a big deal, but now was the time for your future toddler to learn the rhythm of walking. This would require a new kind of balance. Going from one step to the next took a bit of practice joining hand in hand with you.

You kneeled down on the floor in front of your wide-eyed wonderer encouraging a step forward with your voice. In order to learn the balance needed for taking one step after another, you put their hands in yours. For those next few weeks of the waddling process, your toddler did a strange version of the Macarena. You walked in front of him guiding him with his arms straight; his hand in yours as his knees locked with every step. Then his arms went straight up into yours as you walked behind him whispering words of encouragement from overhead. Lastly, his arms went out to his side as you took his hands in yours. He was no longer looking at you face to face, but instead he faced the prize laid out before him—a favorite toy, a cookie, or stuffed animal. Learning a smooth stride complete with the ability to let his arms swing naturally beside his body would take a rhythm and balance that would not take long for your kiddo to master.

As we discussed in the previous chapters, the spiritual foundation of your relationship with your children is to help them discover God's design for life. They are able to live out God's design by learning the spiritual rhythms and balance of a relationship with Christ. Here are the big questions you have to answer:

*How much does my child need to know,
who does my child need to be,
and what does my child need to do
in order to experience an abundant life in Christ?*

There is truth, identity, and action in the Christian life. I can remember as a young child growing up in church learning simple songs about God, Jesus, and the Bible. Those songs taught me about people of faith, the books of the Bible, and how God brought the world into being. They told me what happened to people who trusted in God, how God wants us to love others, and they made Jesus' life real to me as a little boy. I had no idea then how much truth was being poured into my young mind. From the very beginning of my own spiritual journey it has been about knowing, being, and doing. Now I get the privilege of partnering with God to teach the same concepts to my children just as you do to yours.

All of Life Comes Down to Just One Thing

You cannot be the ideal person or live the right way unless you first know the truth. This is the first step in a spiritual journey with your child. I'm sure we would agree that the source of truth for a Christ follower is God's Word. It is the first place we turn to find solace, direction, and instruction for our lives. If I asked you if you wanted your child to know God, you would emphatically answer, "Yes." If I further asked you if you wanted your child to know God's Word, you would even more loudly answer, "YES." If I probed again and asked if you were willing to help your child to know God through His Word, you would shake me saying, "Of course!" Yet what most of us find ourselves struggling with is what exactly does that mean? What am I supposed to teach my child?

Some of us have tried the whole "I'll just open it and read where it falls" technique. While it might work sometimes, more often than not the results can be pretty sketchy. Maybe you have tried the approach of sitting together as a family and reading every chapter in chronological order to your children. You found that it worked great through the epic tales of faith and betrayal of Genesis, then through the plagues, split sea, and manna from heaven in Exodus. About the time you got to Leviticus with all of its stoning of disobedient children and weird diet plans, the wheels started coming off on your family Bible reading time. In contrast, maybe for you the notion of even picking up the Bible to read to your children feels overwhelming like you just won the contest at Costco where they let you pile on anything in your cart for free for ten minutes. As the time ticks by, you wonder, "I have no idea where to start."

One of the most famous American works of literature is *Gone with the Wind*. That heavyweight by Margaret Mitchell has 423,575 words. If you consider great European literature, *War and Peace* by Tolstoy boasts more than 560,000 words. Going back to ancient

Greece, we have Homer's *The Iliad* with 358,020 words. I've read a lot of classic literature, but I did not finish any of these books. As a matter of fact, I've never even touched *War and Peace* because any book that gives me a hand cramp from trying to hold it too long is way…too…big! Topping the scales at 807,361 words, it is no wonder the Bible is intimidating for most people. How in the world am I supposed to teach all of that to my children?

The first book each of my children owned was a Bible. It was one of those picture books with cardboard pages. Somehow the publisher managed to take the hundreds and hundreds of stories in the Bible and boil it down to twenty two-page spreads. How did they settle on those particular stories? What makes them the most important? While flipping through each story, I had one of those "How did I miss that" moments. There were stories about Noah, Abraham, Joseph, Moses, John the Baptist, and other men of faith. Apparently David is really important because he got two stories. They even included a couple of women: Ruth and Mary.

When you see headlines such as "David Kills a Giant," or "Joseph and His Coat of Many Colors" it would be easy to assume that these are the main characters in the story. The part that I missed (and sadly what we miss in most sermons) is that these people are all secondary characters in their own stories. The main character of every story in the *My First Bible* series is God and His son, Jesus. Instead of getting lost in the minutiae of Scripture, the big idea you should camp out on with your child is that God loves you and wants to know you.

Worship musician Charlie Hall wrote, *"All of life; it comes down to just one thing. That's to know you, Oh Jesus, and to make you known.*[1]*"* It may sound like two separate things, but what Charlie is trying to say is that knowing Jesus and telling others about Him all flows from a relationship with Christ. If I could tease that out a little more, all of the Bible can be made very simple for your child by focusing on these three questions: *Who is Jesus? Who does He say I am? How do I follow Him with my life?*

All of Scripture is truth, but it is not all equally important or beneficial for your child, depending on his or her phase of life. If you only have a limited amount of time to invest in your child, are you going to spend that time reading the lineage of rulers in 1 Kings? I think you would agree that an eight year old probably cannot comprehend the nuances of what is being discussed in Song of Solomon. With the few years you have, think through what are the key stories, passages, and principles you want to instruct your child in. The Bible reading chart on HowYouMeantToParent.com has some suggested topics by age for you and your child to read through together. Even as you look at it, ask the Holy Spirit to guide you in what is best for your family.

Our family has been in a habit of having a family devotion time together since our children were little. We aren't legalistic or dogmatic about when it needs to happen or how long it needs to be, but Mona and I wanted our children to grow up knowing that spending time in God's Word together is important.

When they were just a few years old, we usually stuck to the children's picture Bibles they each had and sang Bible songs together. As they got a little older and could sit and listen to a lengthier story, we started reading through a series of books that take children through most of the major action stories of the Bible. It contained more than two hundred stories so we read one a day. Our children enjoyed it so much; we read some of the volumes again. We figured kids love being read to; why not make it a story that matters?

By the time they reached middle school, we were reading books about missionaries and took one day a week to talk about a current event happening in the world. We would use the event to tie back to biblical truth. We talked about everything from poverty, immigration, dictators and rulers, homosexuality, and just about anything else that was a hot topic in the news. These weekly talks helped to shape our children's worldview, as they started moving into adolescence.

We eventually challenged our teenagers to do their own search-es with the purpose of sharing what they were learning as they read passages on their own. Sometimes, the rhythm of our daily Bible time together was embarrassingly full of yawns and distractions. Other times, we were astounded at the questions and comments a verse or concept could provoke. We might pray; we might not. We might play a worship song; we might not. But the rhythm was a predictable part of our day. Even on the days when none of us were overly inspired to comment, we made the effort to connect on a spiritual level.

What Does God Say About You?

Of the three questions about a life of faith for your child, the second one might be the most critical. *Who does my child need to be in order to experience an abundant life in Christ?* I think it's the most critical because as a child grows into the insecure phases of the teen years, it can become increasingly difficult for them to be-lieve what the Bible says about them.

We have gotten to work with teenagers for more than two de-cades. During that time we have had to help teens deal with every problem imaginable. So often we have seen teens that think if they could just change their own behavior, then everything would get better in their lives. If he were more obedient, his parents would stop fighting. If she were a little more outgoing, people would no-tice her. If he were a little smarter, he wouldn't get picked on. They spend much of their time either trying to please others or trying to change a part of themselves. The main problem is that they have never learned or believed who God says they are.

Teens and tweens are prone to spending large amounts of time and energy comparing themselves to others. They pick apart the person God has made them to be, feeling like it isn't as important as those around them. As an example, my wife and I have led many student groups through personality style assessments. All students have to do is answer fifty questions honestly about who they are and what words, descriptions, or situations they prefer. Remarkably, more than 75 percent of younger teens test out to see themselves as the same personality type—fun, outgoing, energetic, and spontaneous. Among adults it is evenly spread across all four of the basic personality types, but tweens end up answering the questions according to who they think everyone else wants them to be or whomever they perceive is the most popular in their social group. In other words, they struggle to be honest and to feel comfortable in their own skin.

As parents who have had the privilege of observing and knowing our children from their earliest moments, we can remind them of who they are. It is one thing to reinforce positive character qualities or praise good behavior in your child. What I'm speaking of takes it to a completely different level. I am talking about telling your child what God says about them in His Word. Help them to see the spiritual gifts, personality, and character they have as a blessing from the Lord.

When our children were little, we began to observe how they played and responded in situations differently with playmates. Even though our daughter was younger, she was more aggressive. She could easily take charge of playtime with friends and she was not afraid to take risks. We began to observe to her, "I think God has made you to be a leader. If you will listen to the Lord, he can use you to make a difference in His kingdom."

On the other hand, our son would rather die than have a conflict with a friend. He was always willing to bend over backwards to make sure that everyone was happy and that everyone was included when they played together. He was content to go along with whatever other kids wanted to do. As a person with introverted tendencies, he doesn't possess the "conquer the world" attitude that others would look for in a leader. But we see such potential in him to make a difference in other people's lives. Several years ago he was having one of those hard days of comparing his value to others. My wife had him read Matthew 5:9. "Blessed are the peacemakers, for they will be called children of God." She said, "You know, when I watch you, it is almost as if you don't have to even try to be kind. It's just something that God does in you. He has made you to be a giver of peace. That is a rare thing that not many people are able to do." His countenance had an immediate change as she affirmed his God-given value.

A great place to start helping your child know who they are in Christ is the "Who God Says I Am" chart at HowYouMeantToParent.com. It contains more than twenty Scriptures for you to share with your child. These are truths about God's children that will never change. When you bathe your children in these truths about themselves, they learn to take joy in who God has made them to be.

Putting Knowledge Into Action

The last part of helping your child develop spiritual balance is to answer the question, *What does my child need to do in order to experience an abundant relationship with Christ?* In other words, after your child has a basic understanding of what Scripture says about who God is and who I am in Christ, she will need for you to show her how to live life with Him. If your children believe that God desperately loves them, how would that understanding change the way they live their lives? How might it change what you do as a family?

We try to keep the Christian life simple for our children. Everything Jesus did came down to helping others know the Father's love and telling them to share that love with others. First, know His love. Then go love others. Even when our children were young, we began to ask them to think about what our family could be doing to live out God's love in our church or in our community. We helped them come up with concrete examples of ways we could love our neighbors and ways we could serve those around us.

Since we are made in God's image, we can reflect His wisdom, His sensitivity, His generosity, or His creativity as we serve. It is not just having head knowledge; we can actually put it into practice as part of the balance required in learning to take those first steps with our children. As you share stories with your kids (even if they are way beyond story time by this phase of their lives), think about what your child needs to know about living God's design as they put their spiritual knowledge into practice. It is sobering to remember how harshly Jesus admonished the Pharisees for failing to use their knowledge of the Scriptures to change the lives of others. "Woe to you, teachers of the law" isn't a phrase most people would want directed at them. The issue that Jesus had against the Pharisees wasn't their knowledge. It was their lack of love put into action.

We have had a blast throughout the last sixteen years watching our children come up with ways to put their love for God into action. They can become just as self-absorbed as other teenagers, but in the times that we stop all the craziness of our lives and refocus on loving God by loving others, we have gotten to see their faith come to life. Their faith is no longer something that we have taught them. It is something they own for themselves and enjoy living out.

We are told in the book of Exodus the reason Moses had to lead the Israelites through the desert for forty years was because the people did not believe God. They did not believe God was who He said He was and that He could do what He said He could do. Because they did not know God, they could not know and believe what He said about His love and protection of them. Since they didn't know Him, it was impossible to live for Him. It was one tragic misstep after another that started with not knowing God.

Most of us can relate. In fact, just about any sin you struggle with is rooted in a lack of faith that God can cause us to live differently. Think about a few basic examples. Why do we lie? We lie because we don't believe God is our protector; therefore, we lie in order to protect ourselves rather than trust God to defend our reputation. Why do we steal or manipulate? We don't believe God is our provider; therefore, we steal in order to get what we need rather than trusting God, or we manipulate a situation in order to make sure our goals are met. Like the Israelites, we must learn to depend on God rather than flounder in unbelief.

Near the end of Moses' life, after the first generation of freed Israelites had died and the second generation was entering adulthood, God prompts Moses to pass the mantle of leadership to Joshua and Caleb. As Moses gives his last speech to the people who would be entering the Promised Land. He starts off, *"Only be careful, and watch yourselves closely so that you do not forget the things your eyes have seen or let them fade from your heart as long as you live. Teach them to your children and to their children after them. Remember..."* (Deuteronomy 4:9-10a). At this point, Moses begins to recount the times they had seen God act on their behalf over the last several years. He lists times when they cried out to God as well as times that they received His blessing without even asking. Moses doesn't want them to forget any of it. They saw it with their own eyes. They experienced God publicly as an entire people group. They ate, they followed, they rested, they were protected, and they marveled. They would need to remember all of it in order to make it to where they were going to live out the next phase of their lives. God had provided food from manna and quail. God had provided direction in the pillar of fire and clouds. God had provided leadership and training. And God had provided His presence. They would need to remember what they had experienced so they could trust God in the new places they would be going.

Part of a parent's job is to help our children remember the things God has allowed our family to experience as He leads us. It is how we learn who God is for ourselves after having heard of Him from Scripture or through other people's experiences. Our kids need us to help them remember what they have seen with their own eyes. Remind them how God orchestrated the events during a family crisis. Remind them how God provided during a threatening event in our nation. Remind them how God answered a prayer for healing, or finances, or direction, or forgiveness. As you see God provide for you in your own journey of faith, tell your kids the story of what happened.

Moses insisted that the people *"impress them on your children... when you sit at home and when you walk along the road, when you lie down and when you get up. Tie them as symbols on your hands and bind them on your foreheads. Write them on the door frames of your houses..."* (Deuteronomy 6:7-9). Do it every day so you will not forget. Do it so your children can know how to recognize God and can fall in love with Him too. Do it as you are living daily life so they learn to serve Him as well. Moses moves the people from knowledge to practice just as you can do with your children.

Two-One-None Principle

When your child was learning to walk, you determined her boundaries, you taught her balance and rhythm by holding her hands; sometimes walking behind her and other times standing her playfully on top of your own feet and walking zombie-like in tiny steps across the floor. Finally, when the moment was right, as you stood her up to face you, you let go. Balance. On your knees, you scooted a few feet from her to see if she would follow. Rhythm. It finally happened. Her first step alone and you all threw the first big celebration of your new toddler's young life.

After that day, you no longer held both of her hands. Instead you walked side by side with her. You walked in the park, through the malls, and down the streets. Everywhere you went you kept one hand beside you in case she needed it. When she was a few years older, as you walked down the street you would stop at the end of the street and point out the stop signs. "When you see this sign, you always stop and look for cars," you would instruct. Pointing out the loud noise coming from the backyard fence, you would say, "Do you hear that? There's a big dog back there. We don't go over there." Everywhere you went you were helping to mark the boundaries for her. Showing her the way to go. Preparing her to manage on her own.

Finally the day came that she didn't need you for the first time. Maybe it happened as you were riding bikes. On her pink bike, training wheels long gone, your seven year old questioned, "Can I go around the block by myself?"

Is she ready for this? Does she know the way home? What if she falls down? The questions raced through your mind. This is what all the hours of instruction where about. She is prepared for this moment and waits for your blessing. She needs this win. So do you. She will do it on her own and won't need your hand to guide her.

The process happens all over again in adolescence. Whenever your child begins a relationship with Christ, whether as early as six or eight or much later into their teen years, they need for you to walk with them spiritually. You act as a shepherd walking behind them, guiding them toward God's heart and teaching them how much God loves them. When they are young believers, your child's heart and mind is wide open and ready to be on a spiritual adventure with you. You get to teach them all of the things we discussed earlier in the chapter.

The way you guide them will change as they become adolescents, but never think that your teenager doesn't want you on their spiritual journey. Teens love people who are just a step ahead of where they want to go. This is why they are so drawn to coaches, small group leaders, youth pastors, college students, and even grandparents. As a rule, teens seek out relationships with adults who they perceive are a little further along the road they want to go down. Admittedly, there will be times when there is tension between you as they are trying to figure out the dynamics of seeing you as an authority as well as a mentor or friend. They need for you to show them spiritual balance and to help them find a rhythm in life situations.

Let's say your teenage daughter asks when she can start dating. Maybe she doesn't even bother to ask; she just starts lining up guys and expects you to butt out of her business. Regardless, as her spiritual mentor, you aren't going to stand aside, wave to the guy, and say to her, "Have a good time. See you when you get home" as she heads out the door on her first date. At this point, she has no idea how she should be treated on a date. What is she supposed to wear? Where can they go? She doesn't know what your expectations are. No one has given her clear boundaries and prepared her to date.

Ideally her dad would be her first date. He gets to walk alongside her to show her what it feels like to be respected and treated with great worth. Dad gets to tell her what a gift she is, how to keep from compromise, and how to judge a guy's heart. This goes doubly for sons and their mothers. Teenage boys know virtually nothing about girls beyond what they have seen on a screen. They know a whole lot about video games, movies, and YouTube. They know they like girls, but don't have a clue how to respect them or talk to them. Mom gets to walk alongside her son to help him see how to treat someone in a car, at a sporting event, in a restaurant, or at a concert. Mom has to explain to her son how to truly appreciate a girl's beauty, how to challenge her mind, how to guard her emotions, and how to captivate her heart. It's up to mom to show him how he can be respected without manipulation, how his thoughts are valuable and interesting, how his sense of humor can delight and entertain without hurting or causing confusion or unnecessary drama in girl world.

Our culture has already done a sad job of telling your son that he is expected to conquer the playing field when it comes to girls. Yet (you already suspect, don't you) that he knows little to nothing about real women. Even if your son has already delved into the world of texting, Instagram, and Facebook, he is not ready to date until you have done some sideline coaching. Let's face it, learning how to have a real conversation with a girl without letting her lead the way into an emotional abyss is going to go much farther than mastering the art of the hair flip.

In contrast, the media has shown your daughter that her best characteristic is her sexuality. Media messages have bombarded her with the idea that unless she is in the elite minority, she is not blond enough, tall enough, skinny enough, or buxom enough to win a guy's attention. But with the right jeans, perfume, hair products, and pout, she can make herself appealing. Or when all else fails, the messages and photos she sends to a guy's cell phone can make a statement that he cannot ignore. Speaking words of affirmation and protection into your daughter's mind and heart should come from Dad first. Giving her a healthy dose of insight into "guy world" can ensure that she weeds out the ones who are unwilling to jump through the hoops to win her heart the way she longs for and deserves.

According to a 2012 survey among college students, young adults are encountering what sociologists are referring to as the death of dating.[2] There is no dating anymore, it's simply "hooking up." Guys are engrossed in internet pornography and distorted relationships, while girls are obsessed with glamorizing and using their sexuality to manipulate people and circumstances. The result is a collision of inappropriate relating styles that leads to shallow physical encounters without commitment or depth.

When your son is old enough to obtain a driver's permit or a permanent license, you don't give him a car and send him on his way with no strings attached. No. Instead, you spend the time it takes to teach him how to properly handle a vehicle. Or at the very least, you sign him up for a class in driver's education. Then he has to pass a written test and a driving test. It's a months long process he has to experience in order to drive.

I thought my relationship with my own father was going to end as a result of my driver's training. He insisted that I learn to drive using a stick shift. The terrible experience seemed to drag on for endless months of jerking and stalling the car. As he walked alongside me through the experience I finally earned the privilege of driving on my own.

Another of our culture's rites of passage is turning thirteen. On that momentous day, your child is officially a teen and can now be a member of the social media world. Instead of waiting for the right time, 52 percent of 11 to 12 year old children lie about their ages in order to be on Facebook, Instagram, and kik. This includes the 70-80 percent of those underage participants whose parents *help them* to get around the age restriction in the process[3]. Not a great way to walk alongside a child through those boundaries that we are trying to mark for them. Surely there's a better way to model integrity, self-control, and delayed gratification for our kids.

The journey you are on to shepherd their hearts, shape their choices, and send them on their way is a very long process. Sometimes it feels like repeated failures mixed with short intervals of success. Sometimes it feels as if they aren't listening to you and aren't open to instruction, just like we all went through with our parents. On other days, God gives you a window, maybe just a peek, into the mature person your teen is becoming. Hold on to those days and treasure those moments to remind you of the purpose of the journey.

The same thing applies to spiritually mentoring our kids. Helping them to find God's design for their lives takes time. It's not done when they walk out the door at 18. It takes repeated failure mixed with short intervals of success. Moral failures will happen. Spiritual highs will be illusive at times. Some kids are more motivated than others, but God can get us all where we need to be. One day, you will be able to stand before God and say, "I have taught this child everything I know about how to love and honor You. Now I am entrusting them into Your hands." Rather than waving good-bye at that point, however, you now run ahead a bit. You have walked alongside them, now you get to run ahead, turn, and watch for them to move forward on their own. In 1 Corinthians 11:1, Paul says, "Follow my example, as I follow the example of Christ." As they follow you following Christ, you are like a cheerleader—their biggest fan—ushering them closer and closer to holiness and wholeness. Watching their first spiritual steps on their own. No hands. Then celebrate.

Chapter 5

Spiritual Balance Happens One Day at a Time

My wife looked out the back window, then with as much control as she could muster, she said in a raised voice, "Go get our son off of the fence before he kills himself."

I joined her at the window to see our four year old walking along the top rail of our picket fence. Without speaking, I knew what she was thinking. Her mind was racing back to when our son was almost two. He was trying to stand on top of a basketball in our kitchen. As soon as his feet came off the ground, the ball went spinning out from under him. His lower body followed the spin of the ball and in a split second he shattered his femur in a spiral fracture. He spent the next two months in a lower body cast.

There are parents who have gone through much worse with their children. In the big scheme of things, it was just a broken leg, but for us as new parents, this was the first time our child was facing something we couldn't fix. To this day, the most difficult moments I personally experienced with Bailey were when they took the first X-ray and when they cut the cast off. The newly trained technician had never taken an X-ray on a toddler and wasn't exuding much confidence. As we turned to leave the room for a brief moment so the X-ray could be taken, he screamed. And screamed. He looked at me with those eyes that said, "Where are you going? You aren't supposed to leave. You have betrayed me!"

Two months later when it was time to get the cast off, we thought it would be a day to celebrate. We would make a quick trip to the doctor, cut off the cast, then go get ice cream. Needless to say, when you are two years old and a man in a white lab coat is walking toward you with a loud power saw, you aren't thinking about ice cream.

Back to the picket fence walk. I could feel Mona's hand tightly gripping my arm as she implored, "Well, go get him!"

After pausing for what felt like a lifetime, I said, "No. He needs this."

"He needs what? To fall and break his leg again?"

Almost willing him on, I said calmly, "He needs it for himself. He has to show himself that he can keep his balance. He needs to prove to himself that he can do it. If he falls, it's four feet. He might sprain his ankle and he will never try again. But if he makes it, for just a few moments, he is going to feel larger than life. He. Needs. This."

By the time I had finished my coach's speech, our son had made it to the end of the fence. He jumped down and made a beeline for the back door. With a racing heart and newfound confidence, he said, "Guess what I just did?"

Each of our children goes through the same process when it comes to growing up spiritually. They have successes and failures. They have seasons where they feel close to God and others where they feel abandoned. Through it all, they have to learn to own their faith. They have to grow into a place where their faith isn't borrowed from you anymore. They have to test it and find it proven to be true.

The only reason why our son was on that fence in the first place was because I had helped him balance on that same fence so many times before. He would walk along while I held his hand. Because we had done it so often together, he had the confidence to do it alone. This is the same way that our children learn spiritual balance.

They need us to walk beside them, to teach them, and to model for them how to daily live with God.

The following principles include four tools you can begin to impart to your children to help them understand the importance of walking with Christ. As you begin to use these tools with your children at a young age, you will see them grow into the man or woman God created them to be. One day they will walk in your door with a racing heart and newfound confidence to announce, "Guess what God just did?"

Getting Caught in the Act

Many moms have discovered that their most meaningful times with the Savior are stolen moments when they have had to sneak away from the rest of the family in order to have some uninterrupted space in their day. Once the chaos of the day begins, there is little time for quietness. The best time for stillness with God can be in the morning before the rest of the house is stirring. These times sitting on the back patio with nothing but a Bible and the crisp morning air are what get my wife's heart charged up for the day.

When our children were young, they had a habit of coming to jump in our bed in the morning as soon as they saw the clock turn 7:00 and they knew they were allowed to get up. One morning when our son was about seven, he came in and complained to me that he couldn't find Mom. He searched every place he knew in the house including the bathroom, which was sometimes his mother's only place of escape from PB&J sandwich smears and Legos. At that point, our five-year-old daughter came in to point out what she thought should have been obvious to the rest of us. "Don't you know by now that Mommy is outside spending time with God?" Now there's only one way our daughter knew with such confidence that her mother was outside spending time with God. She had already caught her a number of times in the early morning in the same place, doing the same thing.

A few years later, I got up to go outside and take Mona some coffee during her quiet time with the Lord. As I reached to open the back door, I looked out and saw our daughter sitting in the hammock with her mother. They both had their Bibles open, sitting in silence and enjoying the day that God had made. It reminded me of Psalm 145:4: *"One generation commends your works to another; they tell of your mighty acts."* From one generation to the next, the importance of connecting with God was being passed down.

Your children need to catch you experiencing God—talking about God, seeking out God, making space in your day for God. Most of our church services separate the family with the children going to one area and parents in another, but at least a couple of times each year, make a point to have one of your children come to be a part of a church service with you. As they sit with you, watch you read your Bible, hear you worship with your voice, and see you give back monetarily out of God's blessing, they will learn to connect with God in the same ways. It's great when they get to see other church leaders, teachers, or mentors, but it is monumental when they get to see how God is real in your own life.

Search Institute interviewed more than 11,000 teenagers concerning how their families connect through spiritual disciplines. The results were less than stellar. Twelve percent of teens said they have a regular faith conversation with their mother and only five percent do so with their father. Among active, church-going teens, nine percent regularly read Scripture with their parents. The current generation of teenagers is struggling to find the relevance of faith in everyday life. Can faith in Christ truly change the way they live in community with people, the way they love others, or the way they give of their time? When you have conversations with your teens about faith, it helps them to see how a relationship with Christ can change all of a person's life.

Looking for Teachable Moments

Teachable moments are those unplanned and unexpected opportunities that God puts in our path in order to impart nuggets of truth to our children. They aren't necessarily long conversations, but they can pack a punch with truth if you use them the right way. You might be watching television, walking around the block, or playing a game with your child, when out of nowhere you see, hear, or do something that causes bells to go off in your head.

When your tween is watching one of the myriad of shows on Disney or Nick Jr. that captivate their attention, have a conversation about one of the character's decisions and whether they were good or bad. Push pause for a moment and wonder aloud how God might want us to respond in the same situation. Watching football on television this weekend with your son, you will inevitably get an opportunity to talk about a commercial that inappropriately objectifies women or glamorizes unhealthy relationships or behavior. Those commercials making light of excessive drinking or partying are created to be humorous and communicate, "life is more fun if you have (blank)." The bikini-clad models selling everything from makeup, cell phones, and dog food make us feel like our lives aren't complete without the product they advertise. Since you know this already, use it as an opportunity to talk about recognizing truth from a lie, how we can show respect toward women, or the fruitlessness of looking to things to fill up our emptiness.

Sunday nights were a time we always looked forward to when our children were younger. Before our lives became crowded with handheld screens, it was easier to control the influence of TV in all of our lives. Almost without effort, we could limit how much time and what kind of shows our children watched. For us that one night a week, more specifically the two hours of TV we watched as a family was from 6-8 pm on Sundays. Our kids would roll on the floor laughing at the silliness of *America's Funniest Videos*, then we would get a little choked up together watching *Extreme Home Makeovers*. Our kids loved the wild and over-the-top rooms they made week in and week out for another unfortunate family. Better yet were the conversations spurred from watching it together. We would talk about the kind of house they would like to live in one day, and how we might show gratitude for what God has given us now. I took so much joy in hearing my children talk about what it means to be a part of a community, how we are supposed to live life with others, and how we can give ourselves in serving others because God first loved us. I knew that every week would be another opportunity for my children to be both entertained and challenged to think deeper about their own lives.

I never expected anything but goodness to come out of our two-hour family TV time. Then one day it wasn't good. We were enjoying another episode of seeing Ty and his crew bring new life to a neighborhood when the show went to a commercial break. I usually kept the remote in my hand during commercials *just in case*. Wouldn't you know it, the one time I didn't have it would be the one time I needed it most. Suddenly on the screen was the image of a beautiful woman crawling on top of a perfectly sculpted man under a red silk sheet. The dreamy music and caressing arms of their two bodies pressed together left little to the imagination of what this advertised show would be all about.

As I desperately searched in the couch cushions for the remote, I could see my ten year old and eight year old staring at the screen. Then just as quickly as it began, the commercial was over. My first thought was, "Do not blow this out of proportion. They don't understand what they saw. Just ignore it. It's over. Enjoy the show." That's when I felt the Holy Spirit's nudge telling me not to miss the moment. This would be our first opportunity to talk with our children on an age-appropriate level about intimacy in marriage. I apologized to them for what they saw, and explained that God only intends for married people to get to touch one another that way. After we talked for a brief time, we went back to watching and laughing together without letting the hiccup along the way ruin our fun together.

The next time you hear a song on the radio describing a relationship that you know is clearly outside of God's boundaries, capture that moment instead of moving on to the next station. The easy call is to move on; the tough choice is to redeem the moment. I have had to make the same choice many times with my own teenagers. My daughter's life is a musical. She connects with the emotions expressed in music and knows a song for every situation in life. There have been several times that we were riding in the van enjoying the moment, when suddenly one of those catchy tunes about love, lust, or something in between comes on. About the time the singer started describing what he would like to do with some woman, Ashlan got quiet and reached for the radio. I flippantly spit out, "Now, why do you think he wants to do that with her? Why would he go and say something like that?" A response of chirping crickets is all I got from her. Blink, blink.

I tried a more subtle observation, "If these people are really in love, I wonder how it makes her feel to hear him say something so inappropriate to the whole world?"

Breaking the silence, Ashlan said, "Dad, do we have to talk about this *every time* a bad song comes on the radio?"

The next series of questions were all met with labored responses.

"Do you know this song?"(Yes.) "Do you like how the song *sounds*?" (Yesss.) "Do you know the lyrics to the song?" (Ye-ess.) "Do you agree with the song?" (I finally got a No.)

We eventually made a joke about how his mother must be embarrassed to hear her son talk like that about women. I told her I knew that she didn't agree with the lyrics, but it's important to think critically about what we hear and see. I brought the focus back to the truth of Philippians 4:8, "Whatever is true, whatever is noble, whatever is right, whatever is pure, whatever is lovely, whatever is admirable—if anything is excellent or praiseworthy—think about such things." The conversation didn't last long, but it was another reminder for her to consider the world she is part of and how her faith intersects with everyday life.

By the time your children get to middle school, they probably know more about the world than you think they do. Don't be afraid to speak matter-of-factly about God's boundaries. Let your child see that you are not afraid to tackle the tough stuff when God lays it in your lap.

One of my dear friends, another Brian, told me about a time he was riding with his boys in the car while driving down the interstate. They drove along without a care in the world until out in the distance he saw a billboard for a local adult strip club. There wasn't anything particularly revealing about the image on the billboard. It was just a woman's face and a few words that invited travelers, "Come over, and play." He knew what the words implied even though his sons might not have, but more importantly it was the look in her eyes that gave him pause.

As the giant image was about to pass out of his view, Brian looked into the rearview mirror and saw both of his sons staring at the larger than life face and her suggested invitation. All he could think was "Don't miss this moment."

"Sons, do you see those eyes? Those are bedroom eyes. Don't believe those eyes. You remember what those eyes look like. If any girl ever looks at you with those eyes, you run. Do not trust those eyes. Do you understand me?"

That was all it took. Conversation was over. Thirty seconds for a teachable moment. Granted, it could have been twisted into a joke over an awkward moment. But this time, it wasn't. The message was clearly passed on from father to sons. I've got your backs. I am going to shoot straight with you. Not everything of beauty is beautiful. Not everything that looks good can be trusted.

Inviting Them Into Your Journey

One of the best (yet most intimidating) ways to help your children learn spiritual rhythm is to invite them into your own spiritual journey. In our western culture we have made the Christian life overly "personal" and private. We talk about having a "personal relationship" with Christ or connecting with Him in your "personal quiet time." Many times we even hear faith described as a "personal issue." Where did we ever get the idea that our faith is so private? It becomes easy for Christians to condition themselves that what God wants most is… me alone. I believe what God desires of each of us is an intimate relationship, not a singular relationship. Yes, God wants to connect with you personally, but for the purpose of showing you how to connect with others. Likewise, Christ wants to love you so He can love *through* you. With that thought in mind, you can invite your child to be a part of your own spiritual journey. You can be sojourners together.

My dad was an avid outdoorsman. When he wasn't working or at church, he was usually out on a lake with a fishing rod or out in the woods in a deer stand. I think more than hunting a prey he just loved being outside. Some of my best memories of childhood are riding in his pickup truck with a pile of rods, tackle, and a bucket of crickets in the back on the way to a lake somewhere. His passion for hunting, on the other hand, was a skill that passed right over me, but landed squarely on my younger brother.

I have never seen anyone who is a better hunter than my brother. There may be other men more fanatical about hunting, but I don't know anyone that is a better shot than Jason. He has a knack for always being in the right place at the right time. As often as he ends up coming home with game, you would think animals walk up to him asking to be taken home. Ironically, he has lot more trophies go than he has brought home. He is like a hunter version of those fishing show guys. They catch the biggest fish, snap a picture, and then let them go. For him more often than not, it is thrill enough to know that he could take the shot if he wanted to.

As good as Jason is at the sport, he would not have gotten that way were it not for our dad. The first time he went hunting with Dad was when he was seven years old and was only allowed to carry a BB gun. The idea of getting to go in the woods while the rest of the world was still asleep seemed like a privilege only real men could do. He even welcomed the bitter cold as a small test of "big boy" toughness. All it took was that first time together with my dad for him to be hooked.

After a long day of searching and waiting, they began to make the trek back to the truck. As they were walking along the path, it began to rain and the trail quickly turned to mud. Jason was walking behind our dad, but as the sky grew darker and the rain got heavier, he found it hard to keep up. Seeing his anxiousness, Dad turned around and said, "Jason, just follow in my footsteps and you'll be okay." Being only seven, Jason took him literally and tried to step exactly where our Dad had stepped. He almost had to hop from foot to foot trying to match our father's longer stride. Reflecting back on the memory, Jason said to me, "That was the first day of my life that I followed in Dad's footsteps. I had no idea I would be doing it from then on every day of my life."

Because my dad was willing to invite his son to be a part of something he loved, my brother ended up being a far better hunter than our father ever was. Not only did our Dad impart the necessary skills Jason needed for hunting, the student surpassed the master. The same is true when it comes to your spiritual walk. As much as you know about Scripture, living for Christ, and being a part of His church, don't you want your child to grow to be an even more devoted follower of Jesus than you?

I want my son to know everything I know. I want him to have all of my tools for life and more. I want him to grow to be a man of his word and a man who follows God into the fires of faith. I pray I am living my own faith in such a way that he is compelled to go deeper with God as well. I want my daughter to know Christ in a way that gives her satisfaction rather than frustration. I don't want her to be duped by the lies in our culture, but instead I want her to know that

God has her best interest at heart. I want her to know everything her mom and I have learned from our successes as well as our failures. I've learned that this takes a great deal of transparency on my part.

Transparency doesn't come easy for us when we become parents. The more you invite your child into your own walk with God, the more apparent your own flaws become. We are so afraid that if our children see our flaws it will somehow undermine our authority in their eyes. Why would they follow me if I were seen as less than in control? That is the lie that keeps your child from seeing that God is at work in you—that you are being redeemed, too. Some days the path together feels like gliding on glass and everything comes easily. On other days, the rains turn the trail to mud, you're bogged down, and your flaws are as glaring as a pimple on a seventh grader's face. Regardless of whether the current season of your spiritual life is easy or it feels like trudging through the mire, when you invite your children onto the path with you, they get to experience a relationship with you unlike any other they will ever have.

You are the only person who plays such a dual relational role in your child's life. You get to be a parent as well as their brother or sister in Christ. Stop to ponder that for a moment. No one else gets to serve your child in that way. Not their youth pastor, not their best friend, not their grandparent, and not their favorite coach or teacher. You get to be a parent *and* brother or sister in Christ. When you look at your teens as having the same Holy Spirit in them as you have in you, it changes the way you see them. When you believe the same Holy Spirit is doing a work in them just like He is in you, it changes the way you parent them. It changes the way you do life together. Now you can see him as a person who you want to guard and coach and champion, not simply because he is your son who you are obligated to raise into a responsible adult, but because you know what it takes to make it as a Christ-follower in this world.

Inviting your son or daughter into your journey with God may feel awkward at first, but it doesn't have to be difficult. Start with simple steps. The next time you are reading the Bible or doing a study, grab your child's attention for a minute, read it aloud to them, and tell them what God is teaching you. Share what you are praying for them, and then ask them to pray for you. Try something as small as, "Would you pray for me today and ask God to help me be more _____. I think that would help me be a better mom to you." Show your child that you want them to be a part of the walk with you.

As your child grows into a middle schooler, they will start to develop their own thoughts and questions about the Christian life. It can be difficult for them to express what they are thinking, but knowing you have a genuine interest can make it easier. Some time in the next week, ask their opinion about something the pastor mentions in church on Sunday. If your question gets a grunted, "I dunno." That's okay. They aren't used to adults asking them those kinds of questions. Keep the conversation going by sharing what you learned that morning that you think might be relevant to them. How did something you heard impact you? Let your pre-teen see you as no longer just a mom or dad, but rather a student like them who is still learning. Maybe during the last five minutes of trying to get through the insane carpool line at school, you turn off the radio and ask if there is anything you can be praying about today while they are in school. You might get a curious stare and eventual, "Um…nothing that I can think of," but they will leave knowing that you are praying for them. Don't let the awkwardness rattle you, but instead turn the tables and share with them something that is currently happening in your life. Tell them about the big meeting, the difficult conversation with a coworker, or the plan you have to put together, then ask them to pray for you while you are praying for them during the day. You don't have to get too specific. This will blow their mind! When they open the door to head into the school, they are no longer thinking about science or math or who they will eat lunch with. All they are thinking is, "Did my mom seriously just ask me to pray for her? Did my dad just say he needs my help today?" In that moment the reality that you are on a spiritual quest together becomes a little more concrete for your child.

Connecting With God in Everyday Life

It is amazing how many disciplines you have taught your children before they even become teenagers. I bet many of them are things you aren't even consciously trying to teach them, yet you have shown them over and over.

You teach them how to eat healthy. Maybe you put fruit out for your kids during snack times. You talk about the consequences of bad eating. You prepare healthy meals. You limit the soft drinks in the house. You do all of this in hopes that your child will develop a discipline for eating healthy on their own.

You do the same thing when it comes to school. When they were little you read to them every day. When they were in elementary school, you did their homework with them. As they got older maybe you showed them some skills of how to study effectively. You made sure they got tutoring from someone else when you couldn't help. You would quiz them before big tests and make sure they knew how to take notes in class. You knew these were skills they would need to make it on their own in high school and beyond.

The same process happens with sports. You showed them how to throw and hit a ball, run a fifty-yard dash, hold a bat, do a cartwheel and a handstand, and so on. You signed up for a certain team or squad. Maybe you consulted a coach or instructor to give them pointers. You assisted them with exercises and drills to help them excel. It's not that you think your kid is going to "go pro" at whatever they do; it is that you want them to develop a discipline for exercise and healthy living.

In these areas of development we intuitively teach our children positive disciplines, yet when it comes to the spiritual life we feel like we don't know what to do. Your children need for you to help them connect with God in everyday life so they will learn to "own their own faith." It does not have to always be something that mom and dad made them do on Sundays, but instead let them learn how to be with God by assisting them on a daily basis. Just as with academics and sports, there are spiritual disciplines you can teach your children to help them grow in their love for the Lord. Praying, worshiping, reading Scripture, giving, and serving are all disciplines that work out your child's spiritual muscles.

We sometimes end up trying too much too fast. Oftentimes, when you read a book like this or hear an inspiring message at church, you decide, "We're going to start praying together every day before school as a family," or "We're going to read the Bible for thirty minutes every day together." The lofty goal lasts for about two days until you crash and burn, and then feel like a failure all over again. If your children are not used to praying with you or reading Scripture together, a thirty-minute family devotion is going to make them squirm in their seats. The key is to start small and simple with a warm-up.

One of our dear friends works for a ministry in our city that serves families who are dealing with the trauma of cancer in their child's life. Diane is responsible for the volunteers who bring meals, clean the guest apartments, rake leaves on the grounds, provide transportation to the hospitals, and spend time with hurting parents.

As great as it is for her to show other adults the joy of serving, she wanted her own children to understand how we connect with God by serving others. From the start it wasn't merely a job; it was an opportunity to bring her family together. Her oldest daughter starting coming to see what the families go through each day. After going with her mom, many times just the two of them, she recruited students from her school to be a part of serving the families. Her younger daughter got her soccer team to help with small projects. Her two boys would often go with their dad to take meals or play with the children. The more they served, the more they asked to go serve. Along with playing video games and sports, serving others has now become one of their favorite things to do.

Diane didn't have to create a new thing for her family to participate in. She started where she was currently involved on her own. She invited her children to be a part of what God was already doing in her life. The spiritual discipline of service is not something she and David have to show their children any longer; it's now a part of who they are as a family. You can do the same thing in simple and small ways to teach your children to connect with God daily. To get you started, I've created a list for you of easy ways to teach spiritual disciplines to your children. Go to HowYouMeantToParent.com to download the list of activities for every age.

Chapter 6

Teaching Them to Fall (and Get Back up Again)

"No matter what, Dad, don't take your hand off of the seat. Okay?" These were the last words my son said as he sat on his bike minus the training wheels.

I started pushing him down the street with my hand firmly on his bike seat. Putting on my best Coach Dad voice, "You're doing great, Buddy. You've got this. Just like you've done every other time."

When the bike was going as fast as I could run, I took my hand off the seat. But it did not matter. He had it! He rode like a champ. The handlebars were secure, the wheels pointed straight, and he had all the confidence he needed. Until he looked over his shoulder, that is. Yep, you know what happened next.

Instead of looking at the road ahead, he wanted to know where I went. It didn't take long until the bike was crashing into the curb and he was sliding across the handlebars. He was hurt, embarrassed, and done with riding a bike. He wanted to stop for the day, but I did the same thing you did when you taught your child to ride a bike. I picked him up and put him back on the bike.

I would love to say this was the last time he crashed. Instead he spent the next hour looking over this shoulder only to wobble and fall again. And every time he got unbalanced, I picked him up, just as you did with your own child.

It's hard watching our children crash their bike when they are four or five; it's brutal watching them crash in things they attempt at fourteen. Even though we mark the boundaries, we always have to let go to see how they do on their own. For the most part, they learn to walk well. Nevertheless, they will have failures along the way. As much as we hate it, they will fall. They lose control, make poor choices, and have to deal with shame, grief, and remorse. Worse yet, they will not always know instantly how to get back up again. This is one of the times they will need you most.

Remember that the foundation of the spiritual relationship you have with your child is to help them discover God's design for life. Everything about the Two-One-None principle leads to that discovery. Falling and getting back up leads to God's design for life. All of it—the successes and the failures—lead back to Him. Parents try so hard to remove difficulties and obstacles from our kids' lives. We want a smooth road in front of our teenagers. We have to keep in mind that for many of us, the greatest seasons of spiritual maturity came during the harsh times. Instead of taking away all of the hurts in life, we must help them to see God during those times. After equipping them with everything they need to get started, we have to open the door to see what happens.

At some point, we move from talking about healthy boundaries in dating to letting our teen go on a date. We move from talking about honoring God with technology to letting them have a cell phone or Instagram account. We move beyond theoretical moral issues that God has addressed in His Word to real life circumstances. Even when your conversations about expectations, integrity issues, boundaries for sexuality, and all kinds of other moral and spiritual matters have gone well, at some point your teenager will experience the same thing that happened when they were learning to walk or ride a bike. They are going to fall. Brace yourself for the inevitable. We hate it and dread it with everything in us, but it is going to happen.

Before you can teach your child how to get up after a fall in life, you have to understand what kind of fall they are experiencing. Not all falls are the same, nor are they all your child's fault. The more you understand the situation, the better equipped you will be to give them the truth they need and to help them see that God is still at work. On any given day, your child can have one of three different types of falls. They all hurt.

1. An unprovoked circumstance

This kind of fall is like a punch in the gut that seemingly comes out of nowhere. There isn't anything that your child necessarily did wrong. On the contrary, it is usually something unfortunate that happened to them. Many times there is no explanation. One night at dinner you announce you received a job promotion and the family will be moving during spring break—even though it's a great opportunity for you, it seems world shattering to your teenager. Or perhaps your ten year old is at school and for some unknown reason a bully decides to unleash her vile threats out on your daughter. Or simply because your son happens to be on a certain sports team, he has to face the consequences of the entire team's punishment for one team member's wrongdoing.

Recently, I read a story about a thirteen-year-old girl whose photo was posted to a porn site[1]. It was an innocent picture of her in a bathing suit from a family vacation. Someone had lifted the photo from her Facebook profile and posted it to an adult site as a teaser picture. A boy at her school discovered the picture and started passing it around to all the other guys. No one questioned her classmate's lack of character for being on the porn site or passing around the picture. She on the other hand, was labeled with a reputation for something she hadn't even done. You can imagine her devastation.

The difficulty of dealing with an unprovoked circumstance is there is nothing to repent from, nothing to make better, and nothing you could have done differently. It just happened. You have to help your child process and respond. Their tendency can be to internalize the situation. In a child's or young teen's mind, this happened because there is something wrong with them. They aren't good enough, pretty enough, or smart enough to have turned the tables in their favor.

You know from your own experience growing up, that your teenager will bear an ample share of unprovoked circumstances. As faithfully as you can, it will be your responsibility as well as your honor, to walk alongside your teen as they face the consequences of being in the wrong place at the wrong time.

2. An unmet opportunity

This type of falling can feel like a mortal wound when you're a teenager. It usually involves the death of a dream or a goal that never quite comes together. Maybe your daughter was looking forward to getting a role in the school play, but she didn't get a callback. It could be your son made straight A's for the first three nine weeks, but earned two B's on the last report card, moving him out of the running for the highest ranking in his class. You remember what it was like longing to be noticed by that one certain someone in high school, and no matter how much you tried, they never reciprocated your feelings.

Any opportunity that your son or daughter hopes for has the potential to be cause for a fall. The longer the dream or goal has existed the harder the fall can be, especially if you've encouraged the dream. Let's say you have been playing football with your son since he was three because you have a dream of seeing him play running back in high school. You've taken him to all the right camps and had him learn from the best peewee coaches, but for whatever reason he makes the team only to place in the shadow of someone who you would have deemed far less athletic than your son. This causes disappointment, frustration, and anger for both of you. He will need you to help him navigate the experience in an honoring and honorable way.

As gently as you can, you will need to be the one to validate your teen's grieving process, giving them space to experience disappointment, anger, regret, and finally acceptance as they face the loss of a hoped for opportunity.

3. A moral compromise

This is the one that parents tend to latch onto with the most anxiety. Whether intentional or unintentional, your teen may choose less than God's best in a moral situation. Oddly enough, more often than not, I find that teenagers rarely set out to intentionally sabotage their lives through moral compromise. They typically do not willfully go out looking for a destructive lifestyle that will ultimately wreck their relationship with you and with other people.

As I mentioned before, I have never met a 16-year-old girl who purposely decides to go to a keg party with the intention of getting pregnant. Instead, there is usually some other thinking process involved. A student who cheats on a test does not generally think through the potential consequences he will face in terms of damaged relationships with teacher, peers, and parents when he chooses to cheat. All he is thinking about is that he has the chance to see the answers he needs for a higher grade. Both the girl at the party and the guy in the classroom were looking for the same thing—acceptance. I'm not excusing the wrong decisions; I am simply saying I understand how it happens. It wasn't always a conscious choice to do something destructive.

That is not to say that it never happens. Certainly, there will be times your child willfully chooses less than God's best. Just like with every one of us, there will be days they will say, "Today I want it my way and I don't care what anyone thinks." Even when you have walked with them through God's design for life in this particular area of integrity or relationships, they may choose a shortcut. Seeing and understanding what God's plan is, they still choose their own way. And then they will face results that are devastating, leaving them wondering, "How did I get here? This is not what I thought would happen."

At spiritually sensitive times during your son's or daughter's fall, you may be able to perceive the intention written in the stunned or grieved expression on your child's face. If they are already experiencing the Holy Spirit's work in their conscience or in their heart, the shock in their eyes is a dead giveaway that they did not think through their actions and probably did not even have a preconceived plan at all. At other times, the mask over their face is a clue to their level of pre-meditated deception or at least the self-protection involved in their thinking process.

Either way, it is still your role to walk alongside the moral failure. More often than not, the way your teen understands how to admit a moral failure and appropriately deal with the necessary steps for admitting wrong, moving toward restoration, and "standing back up," will largely come from the way you respond to their falling and getting back up again.

Bearing the Burden With Them

In any of the three falls, your teen will have to see that you are willing "to bear one another's burdens" in their failure. For example, you will share in their feelings of betrayal and disappointment when it is an unprovoked circumstance, modeling how to take Christ's yoke upon you as you go the extra mile and love your enemies. You will share in the regret of missing a longed-for opportunity or seeing a dream come to an end, willingly drawing near to Christ during a season of grief or anger. And you will face the humbling act of admitting guilt, receiving forgiveness, and making amends for intentional wrongs. You cannot do it instead of your child, but you can do it beside them; walking with them through each step of the process.

Galatians 6:2 encourages, "Carry each other's burdens, and in this way you will fulfill the law of Christ." Just to be clear, it does not say that you are supposed to take over the other person's burden. No, you are to help carry the burden that your teen is bearing. In your child's moral failure, you are not to pay the price on their behalf. Only Christ can do that work. In your child's moral failure, you are not to fix the problem so they do not have to face it. Your child will have to take responsibility for making things right when another person is involved. As much as you might wish to take away the grief, the shame, or the emotions, you cannot. But you can come alongside of them to help share their burden.

Several years ago, my son's three best friends, two of my wife's closest friends, and one of my daughter's friends all moved over the course of a summer. It felt like we were all walking along a relational death zone in our house, wondering what we did wrong. It was a painful experience for all of us watching our friends leave for a job change, school opportunities elsewhere, and to move to a new church. Even though it didn't involve any of my friends, it affected my entire family.

One afternoon during that season I walked into our son's bedroom and found him curled up in his bunk. At first I thought he was sick, but as I got closer it was obvious he had been crying. Concerned, I asked, "Are you okay, buddy? What are you doing?"

"Just praying," he replied in a melancholy tone.

"What are you praying about?"

Choking back tears for a moment he said, "I was praying that God would give me one friend that won't move away."

It was the first time I ever remember seeing my son grieve over a significant loss. This wasn't a broken toy that could be replaced or a lost ball that could be found. It was especially painful to watch because I knew I couldn't fix it.

In the real world, words like "It'll get better" or "You'll make new friends" sound like something from an after school TV special. While the words are true, they are shallow and belittle the breaking of a tender heart. You remember when your parent would say things such as "Oh, this is just puppy love; you'll get over it." Or better yet, "Crying isn't gonna make it any better." Didn't that kind of comment make you feel instantly suspicious? You knew in that moment that your parents were not fully attuned to the hurt you were feeling as a teenager.

My son's experience was one of those moments we all face as parents where we have to resist trying to fix the situation. Instead, we have to choose to just be with our children where they have fallen. I said, "I wish I could bring you a new friend today, but I can't. I wish I could tell you that it won't hurt tomorrow, but it probably will. What I can do is pray with you. Why don't we pray and admit to God that we are not enjoying this and let Him know you are hurting, and ask Him to bring new friends when the time is right."

In bearing the burden when our children have fallen, we have to resist making things instantly better. After helping your daughter get to summer drama camp and practicing lines with her for the fall play, you cannot make things right when she does not get a call back. You can only be with her in the hurt. You cannot drive to the drama teacher's house and demand a role for your daughter. Dads cannot get out of the stands and take over the coach's job when he does not play your son. We are tempted to fix things by manipulating situations in our child's favor, but we must resist.

It's one thing to put a Band-aid on your child's skinned up knee or to hold your daughter when she is grieving over being left out of a group event yet again. But there is a firm line you must not cross between being a good parent and being your child's savior. When you fix your child's every disappointment, mend their friendships for them, or constantly call in favors so your teenager gets a leg up in a situation, you risk putting yourself on a tall pedestal. The fall from on high will be painful for both of you when they realize you are not their savior.

Another temptation parents face when our children have fallen is to remove natural consequences. We all hate seeing our children go through difficulties even if it is of their own doing. Removing consequences from their actions keeps them from taking responsibility, learning from mistakes, and seeking forgiveness from those they have wronged. There is a huge difference between bearing the burden with them and taking away natural consequences. Look at these three situations and consider how you might respond.

1. Your eight year old leaves her bike in the front yard overnight. The next day she goes outside to retrieve the bike and someone else has taken the bike. Your daughter is

devastated. Do you immediately buy a new bike? Do you tell her to wait until her birthday?

2. Your child is in middle school. She is at soccer practice and her coach asks her to run a difficult drill. She is having a bad day and repeatedly snaps at her coach. For her poor sportsmanship, the coach tells her she will ride the bench the next game. Do you have words with the coach?

3. You stay up very late helping your high schooler with a major history paper. Tired the next morning, she leaves the house and forgets to pack her paper. She can turn it in the next day, but then her grade will drop will from a "B" to a "C." Do you ask the teacher to excuse it?

We must say to our children and teens with as much transparency and respect as we can muster, "I wish you had chosen differently. I wish I could fix this, but I am willing to go with you to meet with an official, a coach, or a teacher so you can tell him what happened. If at that point, you want to ask what you can do to make the situation better, retake the test, redo the assignment, or simply face the consequences as they stand, I will be there with you in the conversation." That way, we give options for how a mature person can face responsibility for seeking to make things right together with a trusted advocate. Our teens do not have to feel alone as they learn to get back up after moral failure.

In my role as Spiritual Life Director at a Christian high school, I was frequently in the position of being an advocate for students. I could be a "safe" adult students could talk to on campus without fear of punishment. Every so often, I would be called into a meeting in the principal's office that was initiated based on something a teacher had discovered about a teen where the student's parent was being called in to confront the behavior. It was always a shock to me to witness a parent's response when the student admitted to cheating, or drugs, or whatever the infraction might be. While I am the first to admit it's hard to respond well under pressure in the heat of the moment, it is crucial when it comes to modeling falling and getting back up. Periodically, even when a student was brave enough to admit the wrong, the parent's immediate response was to redirect blame to someone else—the teacher was too hard, there was too much peer pressure, or there were difficult circumstances at home. All the while, the student is hearing the parent's attempt to overrule the natural consequences and avoid any further responsibility.

Surely, there is a way to talk about breached boundaries and moral failure in a way that assigns appropriate responsibility, accepts consequences in a mature manner, and enables the student to begin to stand up again without shifting the blame to someone else. We all have to learn from our mistakes. We all have to learn that our mistakes have consequences. We all have to face the reality that many times our consequences have a ripple effect impacting more people than we thought would be involved. It is the nature of sin. Whether intentional or unintentional, whether a loss is prompted by accident or oversight, the ultimate solution points back to finding God's purpose in life. Christ is the One who puts broken pieces back together and restores wholeness and holiness.

You are not the super hero for your teen. You point the way to the Savior. If I cannot fix the circumstance, I know there is a God who can make all things new out of even our worst experiences. We must call on Him to do the work. When my middle school daughter came home with a number of text messages all leading her to read between the line and discover that she was being excluded from a sleepover, my wife and I wanted to step in and have a pow-wow with the moms involved. However, in this case, we held off. We reminded our daughter of who she is in Christ. She said she wanted to pray about it. We prayed and waited to see how the Holy Spirit would respond in her circumstance. In the meantime, we were with her in the emotional turmoil. When two of the girls apologized on their own, our daughter said she was glad we did not step in.

Even in times of intentional moral failure, I find myself in a position of asking questions of my children. Trying to be as non-threatening as I can, I calmly say things like, "Tell me what happened. Can you pinpoint what was going on in your mind when you made this choice? What kind of pressure were you feeling at the time? What kind of consequences did you think through when you were making the decision? Now that we all know about it, how do you feel God might be prompting you to respond? What might need to happen to make things right with the other person?"

Depending on my attitude when asking the questions as well as my teen's spirit during the process, at times the Holy Spirit may lead us to responses that neither of us would normally think of as possibilities. Glimpses of true brokenness and repentance or a transparent honesty that exceeds expectation might surface. The freedom to express their side of the story or to express anger or outrage over the outcome might actually become therapeutic rather than destructive. Other times there might be only a baby step towards owning up to the wrong behavior, but just as we champion our toddler's first hesitant steps, we can champion the spiritual baby steps in getting back up after a fall.

Five Steps to Help Them Get Back up Again

1. Explain God's pruning process in your own life

Your child has an unmet opportunity—they didn't make the team, they weren't invited to the party, they wanted a certain car but didn't get it, they were rejected by a crush. Instead of insisting that they suck it up and stop the whining, you can share a time when you didn't get something you had your heart set on. Tell them about the time you were so convinced this great thing was going to happen. From your perspective then, God withheld a blessing from you. Looking back you understand that God had a different plan and worked things out for your best interest.

Sharing our own pruning process helps not to belittle the process in our kids' lives as well. Mona and I have each shared deep, broken-heart experiences with our kids from before we were married and thought we would marry other people. I was engaged to another young woman at one time and it was a good relationship, but when the rug came out from under us, I was blindsided emotionally. When God brought the woman who is now my wife into my life, I moved from being forlorn to being amazed with gratitude. Of course, my children cannot imagine another woman filling their mother's role, so they are grateful that God let the first breakup happen. It puts a different perspective on loss when you can see down the road to how the outcome affects your life in a positive way.

When God says "No," it is easier to stomach when you can hear evidence that indicates it might be for a bigger reason. The typical teen cannot see beyond now. This is where you get to step in to help clear the haze. Is it possible that she didn't make the dance squad because God has a different way to use her this year? Is it possible that your son didn't get the job he wanted because God is going to bring a better opportunity shortly? Sometimes God removes things from your child's life that they perceive to be a good thing—a friendship, a college choice, or a summer trip. His purpose isn't to cause pain; it is to remove the distractions from their path so they can clearly see what lies ahead.

2. Invite them into your valleys and mountaintops

The Christian life is a constant ebb and flow like the tidewaters of the ocean that move in and back out each day. There could be weeks or months in which you feel a deep intimacy with God. Other times you feel like you are praying into an echoing cavern with no response. The longer you have followed Christ, the easier you recognize the changing seasons of your spiritual life. Your teenager does not. Most likely, your son or daughter has not learned to live connected to God regardless of what their emotions are telling them. Besides taking your relationship with them to a deeper level of intimacy, when you invite your teenager into your own spiritual highs and lows, they begin to see what a daily walk with Christ looks like. Let them in on things God is teaching you in your life. Whether you are feeling a spiritual dryness or if you and God are rock solid, invite them into where you are.

Even if teens have made a commitment to Christ, the art of abiding in Him is a lifelong process. In our western culture, we talk a lot about Christian maturity and growing in Christ. We use icons of a seedling that will grow into a mighty oak tree to indicate what spiritual maturity can be. We highlight our "mountaintop experiences" when we return from youth camps and spiritual retreats. We champion how far we've come in our walk. However, we seldom talk about what it is like to live life in the valley day to day. I'm afraid this may set them up for a false sense of what the Christian growth process is really like.

We cannot discount the valley seasons when it comes to growing in Christ. We should not gloss over the seedling season as if we are so removed from that part of our development it no longer has any value. We are all still in process with valleys and areas of our lives that have the look of tiny buds. We may feel exhilaration when on the mountaintops, but that is not where most of life takes place. Everyday life happens during the journey or while we live out normal life in the valley. Consider the experiences of several people from Scripture[2].

- Peter, James, and John went with Jesus up on a mountain. They see Jesus' appearance change along with an otherworldly encounter with Elijah and Moses. Then Peter, James, and John came back down to the valley.
- Noah parked the ark on top of a mountain and God made a new covenant with him. Then Noah came back down to the lower ground.
- Moses went up on a mountain where God gave him the Ten Commandments. This happened not once, but twice. Then Moses came back down to the people.
- Elijah had a miraculous experience on a mountain. He humbled the prophets of Baal when God showed up as a blazing fire. Then Elijah came back down to the valley.

The valley is where we do most of our living and abiding in Christ. Our children need to know it's okay to be "not there" yet. Real intimacy with God can happen as a seedling or as a mighty oak. Real living in our broken families means that connecting with God is not always a mountaintop experience. Inviting our kids into our daily rhythm of connecting with God can help them figure out how to walk those baby steps more consistently.

3. Be willing to share your own life mistakes when appropriate

There is no better way for your teenager to see you as a real person than to share your own life mistakes on an age-appropriate level. Of course, your teen does not need to hear about every time you snuck out of the house or acted out sexually or dishonored your parents. They will not benefit from hearing exactly how you achieved a level of deviance but still turned out okay. Certainly, if you secretly retain a sense of satisfaction, pride, or justification for those past sins without appropriate repentance or regret, your teens will notice that and see the hypocrisy there. But at times, admitting a past moral failure to your child can help them to know that not only can you relate and understand firsthand what they are going through, but you also can tell them how God provided a way out for you.

We all have a thorn in our side, do we not? We all have something the Enemy uses to get to us when we are vulnerable. For my daughter, we have learned that this comes in the form of dishonesty. When she is afraid of being hurt, caught, or embarrassed in some way, she tends to lie in order to avoid exposure. It's usually over little things, never the really important moments in life. But it happens. When she was younger, it happened often. We would talk about how important it is to be able to trust each other, and how God's design for life is truthfulness, even how hurt we were about not being able to count on the things she said, but there would be no change in her behavior.

As time went on, my wife began to share times in her life when her own struggle with truthfulness was a problem and how it impacted her relationships as well as her decisions as a young girl. In her case, she had lied in order to make other girls think of her a certain way, even though her stories were untrue. She was afraid they would reject her or that she would be embarrassed if they knew the truth, so she protected herself by lying. At the time, she did not know how to trust God to be her protector when it comes to admitting wrong or sparing reputation. Years after my wife was an adult, the Holy Spirit began to prompt her to go back to those few people from her past to make things right with them over lies she had told them. When she finally tracked down the girls (now grown women), she felt free from those past issues of fear and self-protection. Mona's story helped our daughter see that lies never really leave you until you deal with them head on, but it also helped her realize she was not the only one who battled the tendency to feel the temptation to lie in order to protect yourself in situations. In addition, it helped her to see that there are potential life-long consequences to the choices you make in your youth.

As our daughter has blossomed into a young woman, we've seen her begin to make the tough choice to be honest with us or with a friend. She has seen the freedom that comes with truth and what it means to live life in the open. We've even joked with her at times that maybe she has gotten *too* honest when she shares her feelings with us about the latest cute boy that has come along. (There are times you just prefer not knowing how your girl feels about a cute guy.)

4. Model biblical restoration by being willing to ask for forgiveness yourself

When I was in college, I had one of the coolest retail jobs ever. I loved working with customers, the environment was high energy, and the team I worked with was fun to be around. If there was ever going to be any tension though, it was with our boss. He was young and hip like the rest of us, but also struggled with the same self-discipline issues that we were all trying to grasp as college students.

If one of us came in just a few minutes late, he would write it up and put it in our permanent employee record. Then he would come in late and would make it known he wasn't under the same rule since he was the boss. If he came in with a bad mood, everyone could feel the tension. The boss became, well...bossy. Bossy in a way we didn't want to follow him or listen to him. We just wanted to leave. No matter how often his behavior was less than professional, we never heard an apology. After a while, we learned that for him, stooping down to the hourly employee's level was never going to happen. The saddest part of it all was that there was so much about him that was likable. He was outgoing, had tons of energy, loved making customers happy, and tried to make work fun. Yet his unwillingness to seek forgiveness was a fixed barrier that couldn't be breached.

The same scenario is played out in many of our homes every day. We think that it is our job to point out error and our child's job to admit their wrong to us and to God. However, one of the best ways to model making things right with God and other people is to be willing to humbly admit when you have wronged your child. Honestly, it is a rare week in our house that I don't have to go to a 15 year old or a 17 year old and say, "I was wrong, will you forgive me? You may have been disobedient, but I had no right to speak to you in anger the way I did." Or "I know you were trying to get my attention after dinner and I wouldn't stop looking at my laptop. I was wrong to show you disrespect like that. I'm sorry." I never look forward to humbling myself. I do not enjoy it and it's usually uncomfortable. Nevertheless, I do it because I want to be in a right relationship with my children, and I want to be in a right relationship with God. I want to show my children that this is the way you make things right in a relationship with another person. I also want to make sure they know that in our house, humility is the norm. I want to assure them they will always receive genuine forgiveness from me when they make similar admissions for their own part.

This also helps to remind each of us that God's forgiveness is limitless. He does not withhold forgiveness based on the number of times you fail; instead He offers it freely out of an overflow of grace. We come to God over and over, and He forgives over and over. It is the same with our children. We want them to be able to come to us every time, not just the first three failures. Every single one. The lines of communication are open for the long haul. Our relationship is secure. We will fail, but we make things right and then get up.

Grace is such a foreign concept to us we cannot fathom that God could forgive the same offense repeatedly. Even though I know it's not true, I have found myself at times thinking, "There is no way God is willing to hear me talk about this same albatross of sin for the hundredth time. He must grit His teeth every time I bring it up." If we as adults struggle to truly believe God could forgive us over and over and over again, doesn't it make sense that our children would feel the same way? Even at a young age, they feel shame for their sin. When you seek forgiveness for wronging them, you are modeling for them how to seek forgiveness from the Lord.

> *"Let us then approach God's throne of grace with confidence, so that we may receive mercy and find grace to help us in our time of need." —Hebrews 4:16*

The most important thing you can teach your children about forgiveness is that it is possible only because of what Jesus has accomplished. They don't have to work for forgiveness because He has already done the atoning work. They don't have to be "good enough" or perform for God because Jesus has already made them right with Him. They don't have to feel ashamed to come to God because Jesus is always waiting with arms opened wide.

5. Discipline within the context of a relationship

Effective discipline is tough for parents because when our children are experiencing a moral failure, we can quickly lose sight of the end game by either cutting short the discipline process or being inconsistent with the discipline process. When our children are going through a moral failure, they need us to step in and be an authority—someone that gives them clear boundaries and consequences. But that is not all we are to be.

Parents must intentionally discipline with the relationship end game between them and their children in mind. If we fail to discipline with respect and honor, then we run the risk of impressing the value of good behavior on our teens at the expense of everything else. Ironically, compliance is not the final goal when it comes to discipline. Does that seem strange? Obedience and good behavior are certainly positive outcomes from discipline, but they are not the primary goals when it comes to walking with teens through their brokenness and sin. Take a look at Proverbs 19:20 and 29:15.

> *"Get all the advice and instruction you can, so you will be wise the rest of your life." (NLT)*

> *"To discipline a child produces wisdom, but a mother is disgraced by an undisciplined child." (NLT)*

When your discipline focuses solely on getting your children to stop doing wrong, you run a risk of teaching your children that the highest priority is obedience, or worse compliance to authority regardless of the condition of the heart. Godly discipline imparts wisdom to your children. In the way that you discipline your teenager, does he leave the situation knowing better how to honor God the next time, or does he leave knowing what not to get caught doing next time?

Parents of adult children will tell you they far prefer to have raised children who learned self-discipline and how to maintain loving, respectful relationships than to have raised a good person who knows how to obey without question. Perhaps you see very little difference between the two in practice. In the end, there can be a vast difference in the heart's motivation. An adult child who has learned to develop the kind of self-discipline the Holy Spirit offers as fruit of the Spirit within the context of loving God and loving other people is light years more mature than someone who knows what it takes to look good by altering behavior simply to impress other people.

Moral behavior is only altered at the core of a child's heart by the work of the Holy Spirit. Just as in an adult's life, our actions come from a heart that is being transformed by God's love. Within our relationship with Him, we are loved, forgiven, and set free to receive love, joy, peace, etc. Then we act on the good works God has created for us to do. It is the same with our children. As we see them becoming more sensitive to the Holy Spirit's prompting in their lives (baby steps), we should be able to trust Him to work out the character issues and behaviors as we walk beside them. Increasingly as our teens develop, we become brothers and sisters in Christ rather than authority-parent and child.

Proverbs 12:18 says, *"The words of the reckless pierce like swords, but the tongue of the wise brings healing."* The way you correct your child and the way you talk to your teen should not bring about further moral failure (recklessness, piercing words, and emotional damage), but should bring healing (repentance, freedom, restoration). Some of us had parents who said things to us such as, "What were you thinking? I am so ashamed of you. How could you ever do something so stupid? You never learn. This could ruin your entire life!" Sometimes, it could even be worse. Do you remember how those words hit you? They didn't instill trust in you toward your parents.

Are you cringing? I am. We've all said piercing words out of frustration. The enemy thrives on suggesting new ways to shred our children's demeanor in times of moral failure. As parents, we are flawed and we lose control. In those moments we don't think; we just explode. Sound familiar? I wonder how many teens wish they could echo the words back to us, "I don't know what I was thinking when I lost my temper and talked back to my coach. What were you thinking just now when you lost your temper and yelled at me?" Yikes.

Godly correction and parental discipline should lead to your child's ability to learn self-discipline and accountability. It's not easy on either end of the balance. It's not easy to provide correction with grace, nor is it easy to learn self-discipline. Both require the Holy Spirit's empowerment in our lives.

So there is no confusion, I am not talking about a "touchy feely, never punish bad behavior" style of parenting where you just talk and talk, but nothing ever changes. We have to work hard to check our own heart and motives before we walk into those tough conversations with our kids. Yes, we must confront sin. Yes, we must give boundaries. But we must always make sure that we mete out discipline with a heart that loves and has our children's best interest in mind. Many years ago, Josh McDowell said something profound that has stuck with me to help shape my own parenting.

Rules without Relationship leads to rebellion Relationship without Rules leads to chaos.[3]

Regardless of how it may seem on the surface, your teenager doesn't live to disappoint or frustrate you. They don't get some bizarre kick out of failing in moral situations. It is usually just the opposite. What your child cannot put into words for you is, "If I disappoint everyone around me, but I know that you're still with me, then I'll be okay." Because of this, after a moral failure, you need to make sure that whatever new restrictions or boundaries you put in place are done so out of a heart of love. Always balance the rules you must give with the relationship you desire.

At some point, I've said to each of my children, "I wish with every fiber of my being that you had chosen differently, because I know what this means in terms of the spiritual, social, and emotional consequences. It might be a difficult path ahead to overcome this. Even so, I can promise to be with you in it now, and I am willing to stay in it with you for however long it takes until things are right again." Your child wants to know not just that you care, but that you see a day when things will be right again.

Chapter 7

Launching Into Wholeness and Holiness

Mona and I have been taking our children on camping trips since before they could walk or talk. On our son's first trip we actually stuck a pack-n-play in the tent because he was less than a year old. We both grew up in camping families and love exploring, backpacking, and hiking. But our favorite is rock climbing. Something about trying to conquer a towering rock face is exhilarating and challenging to both of us.

Our kids have been on more rock climbing trips than I can count. When they were little, they would play with friends on the trail while they watched us climb and rappel. As the kids got a little older, I would strap them each into full body harnesses and let them "climb," too. In reality, it was me hoisting their potato-sack weight up the side of the cliff. Now don't imagine us on a 100-ft. cliff dangling our preschoolers from a precipice. We aren't crazy. But even a 25-ft. route is intimidating when you are four years old. My son tends to be very cautious by nature, and he was a little afraid of heights early on. So when he first tried to climb on the side of the rock, he really only did it to please me in a father-son bonding sort of way. He wanted me to be proud of him, so he tried it—at least once—each time we went on a trip. When he was about ten years old, he actually began to enjoy it himself. His muscles were stronger, his fears were subdued after learning how to trust the rope when he lost his footing every so often, and he was familiar with the strategies needed to get a good foothold or handhold in the rock.

On a recent trip, I was unpacking our gear when Bailey walked up beside me and said, "Dad, how would you feel about me lead climbing this one?" The lead climber is the first person on the slab. He sets up the route for the rest of the group; clipping into positioned anchors along the way. Even for seasoned climbers, lead climbing is a very different experience mentally because if you lose your footing, you can potentially take a 10-20 foot fall before the rope catches you where you last hooked into an anchor point. The rope always catches, but not before your adrenaline surges in an attempt to prepare you for the worst.

As I fiddled with my harness, my son had his eyes on the route. Making sure he had considered the possibilities, I said, "You know what happens if you fall. Are you sure you want to do this?"

He responded in his typical thoughtful manner, "Yeah. I think so. I've been watching you do it for years now, and as long as I do it the way you do, I should be okay. I think I am ready to try it myself."

While I got the gear ready, I tried to keep my excitement in check—praying the whole time both for his safety and that it would be a good experience for him where he could make it to the top. We prayed together at the base of the route for God's protection, clear thinking, and the ability to do what he knew how to do. As I watched him tackle the mountain, it was like looking at a younger version of myself placing hands and feet just as I would. Ten years of togetherness set him up to finally do it on his own.

Most parents of adolescents go through an awkward period when they feel like they are going to pull out their hair...or worse, pull out their teen's hair. Expert after expert on teen development will say this is a natural part of the adolescent experience—your teen will pull away from you, there will be tension between the two of you, your teen will want to buck the system and clamor for his or her own independence—making both of you miserable. But I don't know that God intends for you to be at an impasse.

While it is true that our teens are designed for independence as well as self-expression and identity, I believe the best way to experience those things is in a healthy relationship under the authority of parents who are also under the authority of Christ. The burden is on parents to create this healthy relationship while children are young so by the time they enter the teen years, they don't feel threatened by us being a part of their lives (and we are not ready to kill them).

We talked about walking alongside our children as they become teenagers so they can figure out God's best for them. We talked about what to do when they have failures in life, whether intentional or unintentional. We talked about how we help them get back up after a fall or a disappointment. You have no doubt experienced some of that as you've watched your child, even from a young age. But as they near high school graduation, how do you prepare to launch them from your home to live their faith on their own? There are some key things we must do to help older teens to own their faith and prepare for wholeness and holiness as adults. I cannot say this strongly enough. If you do not help your teenagers to see themselves as whole and holy in God's sight, then it may never happen.

You don't need a college degree in Pastoral Counseling. You don't need to speak a prayer language or have the pope on speed dial. You don't even have to know all the books of the Bible. You simply need a willingness to walk in a right relationship with your child in order to show who God says we are and how we can live for Him. Teens need to have a variety of other spiritual leaders beside them in their faith journey, but you are the linchpin.

Remember, we aren't trying to raise good kids or productive citizens. We are preparing our children to live in the real world and to know how all the parts of life work together as they pursue a deepening relationship with Christ. This is at the core of being both whole and holy. When they are connected to Christ (as holy), then they can be the friend, co-worker, classmate, and neighbor God intends for them to be (as a whole person).

By the time your older teen graduates from high school, he or she still has a thousand questions about life. Most of those questions may only be shared with a pillow as they lay in bed at the end of the day. But many of them will be the same life-defining questions we were grasping at straws to figure out when we were their age.

Where do I go to college?

What do I want to major in?

How do I resist peer pressure?

What is God's will for my life?

Who am I going to marry?

Will I be good enough for someone else to love me?

What do I do if I fail?

How am I supposed to make friends?

What does it mean to be my own person?

Does God even care about any of this?

The relationship your child has built with you, navigating life together, is the most important tool they can have to prepare them for wholeness and holiness. It is important to have conversations while your child is open to them so you can help them think through how to live a whole and holy life in each part of their culture. If they are not given answers to some of their burning questions, they won't see faith as something to cling to. Instead, as life becomes more complex, faith may take a backseat.

As a teenager, I was a part of a large church youth group in the mid-South. In middle school, it seemed like there were so many other kids my age that we were crawling on top of each other like bees in a hive. There wasn't much change when we entered high school…at least, not at first. When I got to tenth grade, I noticed fewer people my age, for whatever reason, were still around anymore. By eleventh grade when everyone got their driver's license, there was a huge drop-off in numbers. At that point, the middle schoolers were more than double high school numbers. Then by the time my senior year rolled around, only a handful of us remained.

Every once in a while at the movies or skating rink, I would see one of my peers that used to come to youth group. It is not like most high schoolers have the social awareness to go up to one another and say, "Hey, I haven't seen you at church in a long time. Is everything okay?" But I would wonder what happened. I wondered why being a part of God's community was more important to some people than others. I wondered why, even though we were all crazy busy as seniors, some people let their faith be the one thing they held to while others let it be sacrificed. I wondered if they would ever be back again. I would guess if you grew up involved in a similar church, chances are you remember the same scenario being played out in your experience.

After graduation, if you were still attending church, you were probably in a very small minority of college or career-minded students still participating in a faith community. For whatever reason during those later teen years, the wheels began to come off when it came to spiritual matters. By the time we got to college or started a full-time job out of high school, precious few of us had an intimate relationship with someone else who was pursuing a relationship with Christ. The sheer number of us that became spiritual drifters is quite sobering.

A recent study concerning the spiritual beliefs of young adults who grew up regularly attending church, shows that among those who called themselves Christ-followers in high school, 29 percent feel less spiritually connected to anything as adults[1]. About one in three young adults feel less connected to Christ, less connected to church, and less involved in their faith than they did five to ten years earlier. More than half (57 percent) attends church less often as an adult than they did as a teenager. Almost 40 percent of them said they have gone through a season of serious doubt about their faith. Sadly, more than one in four admit they no longer embrace their faith at all.

Fuller Theological Seminary and the College Transition Project conducted an exhaustive study on why some teenagers continue to grow in faith after high school while others drift away spiritually[2]. Interviewing more than 500 high school students that were part of a faith community, researchers tracked these students through their college and post-college years. They discovered that 40-50 percent walked away from their faith during college. Among those who shelved their faith, roughly 20 percent said they had intended to walk away to begin with. More breathtaking was the remaining 80 percent who had a disconnected faith but had no idea why they spiritually drifted. Students had started college confident that they would live out God's plan for themselves after high school, but when real world obstacles came or their faith was challenged, they felt their faith begin to fall apart.

Let's get a little closer to home. Perhaps your teen is currently involved in a church youth group of peers who are all intentionally plugged into community together on a regular basis. These students participate in a small group, they go to Sunday School or worship each week, and they even volunteer with VBS or missions trips each summer. According to the studies we just looked at, half of the students in your teen's youth group will walk away from their faith after high school. On Senior Recognition Sunday at your church, it is a disturbing thought that many of those students would already be intending to drop their faith experience over the next few months, and many others will begin to spiritually drift in spite of their good intentions. If history repeats itself, they will not see it coming, and they will not know how they get so far away from their faith.

As a parent of two teens, I want better than a fifty-fifty chance that my son and daughter will make it through college with their relationship with Christ healthy and whole. I have to believe you would say the same thing. Let's think about this. If there were a fifty percent chance your teenager would have a life-altering car wreck, would it not change your conversations about driving safety? If fifty percent of all high school girls got pregnant before graduation, would it change how you talked to your children about sexual purity? If the likelihood of your teen walking with Christ after they leave your home is only fifty percent, what are you going to do differently in the training process?

Paul told Timothy, *"Follow me as I follow Christ."* This is how it happens. This is the answer to your children staying on the spiritual courses they have chosen for their lives. When all of the distractions of the world press against them or compete for their attention, you are ahead of them like an air traffic controller waving warning flags. With every new temptation or trial that comes along, you keep saying to your teen, "Don't lose sight of the prize. Don't take your eyes off the goal. Keep following me because I'm following Jesus."

I was meeting with a father of three adult children one day over coffee to ask him about his experience with parenting. He was further down the road with two married and one in college. He managed to raise three children into adulthood that were all still healthy Christ-followers. This is someone whose experience I could learn from. We swapped stories of all the things we've taught our children, the crazy things they have said that made us laugh, and the pain we endured watching them make foolish choices from time to time. As we meandered through our father journeys together, I asked him several questions. I wanted to know if he would do anything differently. I wondered if his children ever defied his authority or bucked the system. How did he keep them from shutting him out? When I asked him if he ever saw any of his children questioning his beliefs and walking away from him as a parent, he got very quiet as if drifting off to a memory from years earlier. When he finally looked up after seriously considering my question, he replied with a very humble, "No."

This man had never considered the 50-50 statistic as an option for his children. He never forced them to embrace a certain code or adhere to a standard set of rules. He did not leave spiritual training up to a youth pastor, Sunday School teacher, or coach; he made sure he was the primary influence. He lived face-to-face and eye-to-eye with his children all the way through their teen years into adulthood. He followed Christ and invited his children to follow him until they were ready to walk with Christ on their own. He never considered it an option *not* to be involved in the spiritual shaping of his children.

It's unfortunate those conversations are unusual. They don't have to be. Regardless of where you are in your spiritual journey with your children, you can choose to do it differently from now on. Out of my conversation with this father and many other parents over the years, I want to outline three principles that I have seen as common threads in their lives.

Create a Web of Influence in Your Child's Life

God does not leave you alone in raising your child. While you are the greatest influence in your child's life, there are others who should also play a part in their spiritual shaping process. You are the all-star in your child's life, but throughout the journey, you will need to bring in your pinch hitters. If you are living in spiritual community with other believers yourself, then God has given you a shortstop to back you up at third base when the ball is coming your way. You have access to a team of auxiliary players who also have influence in your teen's world. These people aren't merely grandparents, coaches, youth pastors, scout leaders, and teachers. They are part of the web of spiritual influence in your child's life.

When I was in high school, I had a great youth pastor. He did all of the typical things you think a youth pastor is supposed to do—took us on mission trips, hauled us to summer camps, and led Bible studies. More than that, he took a personal interest in my life and my best friends' lives. I remember many long conversations in his office or in the gym. As a young man asking hard questions about faith, my youth pastor was always there to back up what my parents were teaching me at home. After I graduated, he and I would continue to connect every few years and were able to quickly jump into spiritual conversations. Years may go by, but whenever he and I connect, he still asks about my own ministry. Since those early years of my faith, there have been many other pinch hitters the Lord put in my life as part of the web of influence in my faith.

I realize this may not have been your experience growing up, so you will be starting something new for your own children. Begin to look and pray for men and women of faith and integrity to speak into your children. Be willing to go to them and ask them to spend time with your family. Take some time to think about the skills, knowledge, and character traits in these people that you would want to see God grow in your children. Proverbs 19:20 says, *"Get all the advice and instruction you can, so you will be wise the rest of your life"* (NLT).

As the web of influence grows in your child's life, undergird these people with your prayers and your affirmation. Tell these people how much you appreciate the time they invest in your child. Let them know it is a big deal to you that they give of themselves, and note the difference you see in your child. Every year, my son and daughter have had a different small group leader at church. I want those men and women to know I value the time they spend with my children and that their lives are rubbing off on my children. A couple of years ago, I hand wrote notes to communicate my appreciation. Other years, I have simply prayed for them to be the people of God that my kids need them to be in their lives. Many times I stop individuals at church and tell them what a gift I consider it that they are speaking into my children's lives. I am grateful my son and daughter learn from older men and women of faith. They are a select few that God uses in the web of influence.

You always hope that your child will come to you first in a time of crisis. Even in the best of parent/child relationships, there will be occasions where your child may want to bounce something off someone else first. Encourage those relationships with your teenager. Let them know they can always come to you, but you want them to have the freedom to talk to godly coaches and teachers, youth pastors and volunteers. In those unfortunate times when they do fall and you cannot catch them, it's good to know your child has a web of influence ready to help pick up the pieces and get them back on the right path.

See Their Passions and Abilities as Part of God's Plan

What your teen wants for his or her future is probably not clear. They may have a few general ideas or nothing at all. When they get their first real job out of college, the picture can start to clarify itself, but a feeling of lack of purpose can linger. In fact, twenty-somethings typically see a big disconnect between their faith and their vocation. They may see a career as what they do with their life, while they see their faith as a personal component that takes place on Sunday mornings. Because they see vocation and faith as separate issues in life, they struggle to see faith as anything other than a once-a-week event. They don't always see career, passions, abilities, and dreams as part of God's overall plan for their lives.

My son went to a college fair to get an overview of possible colleges in our area. After walking down row after row of booths lined with university banners and reps glad-handing him, he came home more perplexed than before he left. He was even a little depressed over not knowing for certain what he was supposed to do.

"Dad, what if I'm supposed to go into ministry, but I don't? If there is one college God wants me to go to, what if I pick the wrong one? Shouldn't I know by now what I want to major in?" These questions were just a few of his stress-induced sentiments that night. So many unknown factors, potential failures, and uncertain futures made him paralyzed and unable to see clearly. The notion that our teens are supposed to somehow discover "God's will" for their lives before they can do anything is unnerving...and unbiblical.

Our school systems have somehow convinced students that if they don't have life planned out by tenth grade, they are going to miss the career boat. All of the talk about what do you want to do misses the bigger question—who does God want you want to be? When God spoke to the nation of Israel in Micah 6:8, He said, *"O people, the Lord has told you what is good, and this is what he requires of you: to do what is right, to love mercy, and to walk humbly with your God"* (NLT).

I love the way Eugene Peterson puts it in *The Message*:

> *But he's already made it plain how to live, what to do,*
> *what God is looking for in men and women.*
> *It's quite simple: Do what is fair and just to your neighbor,*
> *be compassionate and loyal in your love,*
> *And don't take yourself too seriously—*
> *take God seriously.*

It is freeing to remind your child that God cares about their passions, their abilities, and their dreams. He wants to use these to help them to be a person who is just, compassionate, loyal, and humble. The person God made your child to be is a fascinating pursuit of discovery, and far more rewarding than any career. God wants to use who they are to make a difference for His name.

As my son grapples with his future, I want to remind him that the One who made him is the One who can help him to maneuver each step of the way into a satisfying future—whether that is in a career, a ministry, or any of life's big decisions. The same goes for your children. He already knows their interests, their ACT score, their spiritual gifts, and even what their tuition needs will be. He is the One who will bring them to the places they need to be in order to fulfill their calling and their lives. Regardless of what careers they choose, God can help them live out their lives to glorify Him.

Ephesians 6:6-7 says, *"As slaves of Christ, do the will of God with all of your heart. Work with enthusiasm, as though you were working for the Lord rather than for people"* (NLT). Would it be a surprise to your teen that this verse was not written to pastors? The Apostle Paul is not talking to another young missionary telling him to give it all he has on a church staff or missions organization. Instead, he is talking to lay people who are young believers in the church body. Actually, many commentators think Paul was talking to slaves about their temporary roles under an authority that they may or may not have chosen for themselves. He tells them to do everything to the glory of God.

If your teen becomes an accountant, encourage him to use his analytical skills to the glory of God. If your daughter goes into the medical field or the fashion industry, talk to her about how to do it as a blessing to God and as a service to other people. If your son wants to be a long-haul trucker or graphic designer, help him dream about how God can use him in his pursuit. Any long-term profession or short-term job can be a mission field leading your teen closer to becoming who God intends. Faith is very much a part of what we do in our daily routines, not merely what we do on Sunday mornings. All of life is meant to be lived to the glory of God.

Foster a Dependency on Christ and His Church

When your child is little, they come to you first to make everything right. If he cannot find his shoe, your son plops down in front of you. If she cannot get the peanut butter jar open, she sits it in your lap. When a toy breaks, you whip out the super glue and put it back together. The times she is left out or friends treat her unfairly, you are there to soften the blow with homemade cookies and ice cream. Even as they develop some independence in adolescence, teenagers still say they trust their parents more than other authority figures in their lives. From flat tires to hurting hearts, you are standing at the ready. This is part of your job as a parent and you do it dutifully. Another part of helping your teenager through life transitions is to help them see that God cares about and wants to use their life. Through the glory and the gore of being a teenager, your child has to learn and understand that a relationship with Christ means having a dependency on Him. He is the One who ultimately provides for our needs—financially, emotionally, physically, as well as spiritually.

When we started in ministry to families on a full-time basis, Mona and I sat down with our children to let them know that this first Christmas with no regular salary might be quite a bit different. We made sure they understood they would still get presents from their grandparents and extended family, but our gifts to each other would be limited because of the new journey that God has us on. Our kids were only three and five at the time so they nodded and said "Okay," but I don't think they fully understood the reality of what Christmas morning might be like. At the time we didn't tell anyone about the conversation with our kids and how tight things were. God knew. He provided. When we got home a few days later, we discovered a giant bag at our front door. Inside were four wrapped gifts for each of our children and a few for Mona and myself. To this day, we don't know who God used to provide for us, but He did it in abundance. So we talked with our children about what God did and how He provided when mom and dad could not.

A couple of months later, God surprised us again with bags of groceries on our front doorstep. Our habit had been to buy everything we need once a month and making it last throughout the month with careful planning and preparing freezer meals ahead of time for the end of the month. This was the end of a month with an unusual number of friends visiting and guests coming over. We were getting down to the "I wonder what you use this for" cans left in the pantry. You know, the stuff you throw all together and make a casserole out of. Again, we did not mention our need to anyone else but God, and He provided. We began to approach our financial needs a little differently at that point. We started paying bills with gratitude for God's provision rather than annoyance that another bill was due. My attitude toward cashing a paycheck changed when I knew exactly where the revenue had come from. It was a subtle change, but it was profound. We were amazed at how intimately God understood and met our needs. We wondered if He wanted to be even more involved in our lives through His provision. So after making ends meet on a very tight budget and supplementing only when absolutely necessary with money from our emergency savings, we began to pray before making any unusual purchase to see if God would first provide another way. Sure enough, He did. We needed a new dryer so God showed off and sent both a washer *and* dryer. When we needed a vehicle to travel to speaking engagements, God provided one with plenty of room for all of us to go on long trips together—with a DVD player to boot. What extravagance! We prayed about school uniforms, extra-curricular activities, and routine medical or dental visits. God provided for each one. Sometimes He provided a little extra money to cover this or that, but many times He provided just the right person to meet just the right need as it came up. Each story is precious and significant to us because it is a reminder of how God orchestrated a way for us to depend on His provision and to see His activity on our behalf.

In almost every case, we shared the experience with our children. Many times, I think parents fail to include their children when they go through lean times or struggles because they don't want to cause unnecessary worry or anxiety in their children. If children never see when there is a need, they don't get to experience the joy that comes when God provides an answer or blessing for your family. In fact, when God prompted someone to give us the minivan to replace our old one, we asked our children what they thought we should do with the old one. We thought about selling it to use the money for other needs or even keeping it as a backup vehicle. After thinking about it and praying about it, one of them suggested that we should get it fixed and then give someone else the fun and excitement of getting a van, too. A few days later, that became a reality. God made us aware of a friend that was driving his compact car around his inner-city neighborhood picking up Sudanese refuge children and bringing them to church. Out of nowhere he says, "If I had a van I could pick up so many more kids for church." In a matter of days, God provided not just to our family, but also through our family. I was over the moon watching my children being generous because God had so richly blessed us.

Over the last 10 years, our children have learned to anticipate how our family might be a blessing to someone else's family in the same way—with clothing we can pass on, meals or groceries we provide, or toys and sports equipment that some other child could use more than us. Whenever we drive past a certain exit on the interstate, our children know to look in the back of the car for a granola bar and water bottle to pass to whoever is standing on the corner holding a sign. Encouraging our children to look for God's hand in meeting our daily needs has caused them to be more sensitive to other people's needs and to see how we might partner with God in meeting those needs as well.

Do not rob your children of the joy of being included in a hardship your family can face together as God provides. If you lose a job, need a car repair, or face a disappointment, consider how you can include your children at an age-appropriate level in the process of waiting on God to provide. He is the One they will need to depend on as adults, so we must show them what it's like to depend on Him as they are growing up.

In John 6, Jesus teaches about some hard things. Near the end of His message, Jesus says the words He has been speaking are life giving, but some of the people do not want to believe Him. After He finishes it reads, *"At this point, many of his disciples turned away and deserted him"* (NLT). In that moment, Jesus turns to His twelve core disciples and asks if they plan to leave as well. More than a year into His public ministry, these twelve have seen countless miracles and heard Jesus' messages repeated from town to town. He had warned them that they might not have a place to put their heads and may have little to eat. In fact, Jesus had warned them not to take anything with them. Furthermore, He had challenged them to leave behind family, homes, and careers. So how did they respond to His pointed question? Peter says, *"Lord, to whom would we go? You have the words that give eternal life. We believe, and we know you are the Holy One of God."* Their faith had been put to the test and their conclusion was that Jesus was the real deal.

In the same way, one day your teen is going to go off to college or into a full-time job. They will go through their first real difficulties on their own. They will face people who offer them shortcuts, credit options, vices of all kinds, or relationships that will seem on the surface to be an answer to a significant difficulty or need. We want our adult children to be able to say with confidence, "I know Who provides for me." We want them to be able to recognize the difference between an authentic solution and a false one. We want them to be able to respond to any enticement with, "I don't need what you are offering" because they know how satisfying it is to wait until God provides the real thing. To whom else would they go?

Your child hasn't gone through the life transitions you have lived through. You remember those lean years when there was very little in the way of finances left over. You remember the lonely times when there was no friend to stop by and visit. You recall the hard times when it felt like God was silent. As much as you do not want it for your adult children, you know they will have to go through similar circumstances so God can show Himself to be true to them. They will have to learn the principle of remaining in Christ when there is nothing else. In John 15, Jesus speaks in the upper room with the eleven remaining disciples during what will be His last night with them. Only He knows the unspeakable horrors their eyes will see over the next twenty-four hours. Their lives are about to unravel, but Jesus says to them:

> *"Remain in me, and I will remain in you.*
> *For a branch cannot produce fruit if it is severed from the vine,*
> *and you cannot be fruitful unless you remain in me.*
> *Yes, I am the vine; you are the branches.*
> *Those who remain in me, and I in them, will produce much fruit.*
> *For apart from me you can do nothing" (John 15:4-5, NLT).*

While they are walking close by you on a daily basis, you have the opportunity to communicate to your tween or teen that all of life comes down to his or her relationship with Christ. Many of your child's friendships will change over the next few years, their school environment will change, their emotions will be unpredictable and undependable, but you can say to them with confidence, "God will not abandon you. Lean on Him." In all of the changes, the God of the universe wants the kind of relationship with your teen that will not fail. As a parent, you can admit to feeling nervous about what may come along in your child's life, but God will not be nervous. He knows.

As your teen nears adulthood, he will make decisions that will affect the trajectory of the next decade of his life. You can remind him that God is trustworthy. God will provide a way for the future. Continue to point back to who God is and what He has done. We have already discussed how common it is for us to see our faith and relationohip with God as simply one of many parts of our life. We sometimes fail to see how all of the parts interact because our view of life is like these boxes.

We see our faith as just one of the many parts of life. In this worldview, everything fits into a box and serves a quantifiable purpose. This is why our generation saw faith as something we participated in as part of a church service on Sunday morning. When that activity was done, we moved on to other boxes. We would participate with our family to celebrate Christmas or we might enroll in college to take a class. This is also why it was so easy for us to play games when it came to faith. If we played our cards correctly, we could pull it off for a couple of hours on Sunday mornings that everything was okay.

There are two problems with this worldview. One, if none of the boxes are connected, then there is nothing that holds all of the pieces of our lives together. There is nothing that gives purpose or meaning to any of the parts outside of each part. Since each box's purpose is temporary, the moment it no longer seems to work, we discard the box and look for something else to fill its place. Surely you have encountered people who have said, "I tried that whole church thing in high school, but it just didn't work for me." Many of us can look back and see the traps in our own past when we put all of our eggs into the basket of career, money, or getting a degree. After spending years of energy trying make one box work, we felt like a failure and gave up on that part of our lives.

The second problem is when there are glitches in our boxes that are out of our control. This can quickly lead to anger, resentment, or disillusionment with God. Some of us have the painful memory of parents sitting us down at the kitchen table and basically saying, "We quit. Pick who you want to live with." After years of trying to figure out why, you are still disillusioned with your parents' divorce. Maybe you begged God to make them stay together and when they didn't you were disillusioned both with them…and with God. Obviously, marriage doesn't work, discard that box. Others of us struggled through the college years with one bad relationship choice after another. What we thought should have been a fun time in life left us angry at ourselves and the opposite sex. We swore off dating and friends and we wrote off God, too. I could keep going, but the problem with any of these scenarios is that God was never part of these areas of our lives. He was just another factor that didn't connect to any other part. He fit nicely in our God box.

Instead of life boxes that have no overlapping purpose, show your child a worldview that looks more like this. Even better, imagine the lines blurring and overlapping between family, church, friends, career, finances—all coming together under God's influence, provision, and the umbrella of His direction.

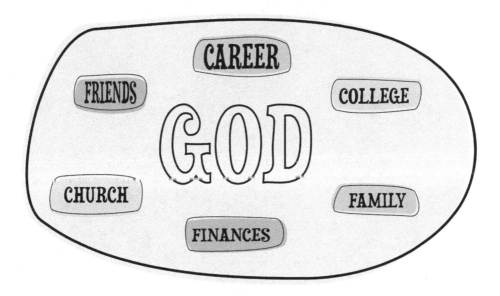

God is the One that gives purpose and meaning to our relationships. He is the One we live for in college. He is the One we honor with our finances and career. Living the character of Christ in our job is a far more eternal reward than another career advancement. Even when your adult child makes mistakes in relationships, God wants to help them navigate those waters and find emotional health. When things are tight financially and things are not looking good for a quick solution, God is ready to be in it through the complications and confusion. **Help your child to see that God doesn't fit into a box; He is the box that holds it all together.**

It is my hope that our children will experience God in a different way. Perhaps they will not limit God to a box that is only opened on Sundays. Maybe they can look at their lives in high school and see God at work in the day-to-day. In their dating choices, in their integrity challenges, and in their technologically-driven world, I am hopeful that God will begin to inhabit more and more spaces of what makes up their faith. Even when the pieces seem to crumble around them, I am hopeful you and I can raise our children to remember who God is and to remain in Him.

Chapter 8

Parenting for a Lifetime

Recently I read an article in the *American Journal of Pediatrics* highlighting a study on parents with newborns in the birthing room.[1] In particular, this study focused on how new babies responded to their parents' faces in the first moments of life. As part of the study, the father would make facial expressions and hand motions in front of his newborn infant during the first moments of life. Now, obviously these babies have never seen their parents before, they have never seen facial expressions, and they don't know how to identify a smile or a nose or eyes. Yet when a parent made facial expressions, the babies would begin to mimic the expressions. The conclusion of the study suggested that children are hardwired from birth to mimic a parent's behavior. Fascinating. Mere hours after a child is born, he or she begins to follow the parent's leading.

In another study from Yale University, researchers wanted to know if a young child would mimic what a parent did if the child knew the behavior was unproductive.[2] A couple of five-year-old children were each given a box that held a toy they could play with. The children were to figure out how to open the boxes by themselves and then determine how the object inside could be played with. In a later session, a parent was in the room with each child when the box was offered. The parent was instructed to sit down with the child and show how to open the box. However, the parent's way of opening the box would intentionally take longer and would include the use of tools like sticks or tongs requiring awkward motions and

techniques. Inevitably, even though the children had already figured out a way to open the boxes themselves, they began trying
to follow the parents' methods for opening the boxes. For better or
for worse, the children opted to do things the way their parents did
it. Even in a fruitless act, the children still wanted to use the same
method a parent had used.

The same thing applies with our teens—the way they handle
their finances, their relationships, the workings of their own marriage, their understanding of who God is and of how to have a relationship with Him—are developed first and foremost after the way
parents do life based on the way parents have understood those
things. Adult children will frequently tend to default to how a parent has modeled a particular life skill. We see it in health as well as
in moral choices. In a study done concerning food and healthy diet,
researchers found that parents who eat a low-fat diet are five times
more likely to raise children who eat healthy themselves. Obesity
is a serious issue in our culture. What does that say about our habits as parents? A simple indicator of whether or not we will have
healthy children may be to take a look at how healthy we are as
parents.

Another study on smoking and tobacco usage showed that parents who smoke tobacco products are four times more likely to raise
children who also smoke.[3] A similar study with respect to alcohol
showed that by the age of 17, 51 percent of teens have seen one of
their parents drunk.[4] Calling attention to these trends is not meant
to make parents feel offended or judged unfairly, but we have to be
willing to take responsibility for the habits we model for our children. You are the greatest influence in your child's life from birth
into adulthood.

Similarly, scientists say that parents are the ones that teach children social norms about the appropriate way to behave in public.
When asked about the most important social norm, parents agreed
that honesty leads the list. Across the board, 100 percent of parents
said that in early childhood development, honesty was the most important value to instill in their children. Likewise, when teens were

polled, 98 percent agreed that honesty is essential to a healthy relationship. Furthermore, 96 percent said that lying is morally wrong. From these numbers, researchers can confidently conclude that lying is a big deal with both adults and teens. However, in practice, right at 90 percent of those same teens admitted to seeing their parents lie. Ouch.

We've all heard the annoying adage, "Monkey see, monkey do," and the equally annoying, "Do what I say, not what I do." While we may not like these phrases, the truth remains that the easiest way to undermine our goals for our children is to model a false way of life. Our children pay careful attention to our actions. They are always watching how we live and what we say. It doesn't stop when they reach eighteen, go to college, move out of the house, or get married. One day they will be in their forties with their own children and they will still be watching you. This is why we never really stop being parents.

Parenting the Hebrew Way

Unfortunately, I think what happens many times in our Western culture is we are preprogrammed by our culture to think that our parenting life span is eighteen years. So everything you want to teach your child about living an appropriate lifestyle—living a life of integrity, having healthy relationships, working hard, understanding sexuality, knowing how to forgive others, connecting with God daily—has to happen within the first 18 years. After that, you are done parenting and it is time to plan for retirement and grandkids.

Most parents of high school graduates talk like that, do they not? I frequently hear comments like, "I can't believe we're almost done" or "If we can just get one more kid out the door" as a high school senior approaches their 18th birthday. Likewise, our teens say things like, "When I turn 18, I'm out of here." Since my own daughter was twelve she has been saying, "I hope you guys are not planning on me being around after I graduate. I'll still come to visit, but I'm not sticking around." She doesn't say it out of any kind of resentment. She is simply ready to blaze her own trail, and I want that for her. However, if we aren't careful, it is easy to start counting down the days until "we're done." If we turn off our parenting radar when she turns eighteen, then we are sure to miss a blessing. She will, too.

We tend to view our role as a parent as either a sprinter or a marathon runner. A sprinter puts all of his energy into a quick burst. It's exhilarating and action-packed for about twenty seconds and then the race is over. A marathon run requires endurance and a steady pace. Participants never run as fast initially, yet they have a consistency that is dependable throughout the course. Either kind of athlete can win a gold metal, but only one will allow you to compete throughout your whole life. You rarely see an athlete sprint racing into their thirties. Sprinting is for the young and fit. But if you watch a marathon, you'll see people in every age bracket, up into their seventies. Parenting is the same way. You can give all you have to your children for a few years, turn in your track shorts, and start planning for your beach house. If you do, you give up a lifetime of influence, training, coaching, and the possibility of affecting the lives of those in your family for generations to come.

Parenting like a marathon runner will require you to cast off some preconceived ideas of the role of a parent. It may mean setting aside western culture thinking about parent/child relationships. You will have to learn a different pace and prepare to adapt to different roles at different seasons in your child's life. If you could parent your child in such a way that you actually gained influence the older they got, would you be willing to do that? If you could parent in such a way that your child saw you as an advocate and partner with them as they grew into adulthood, would you be willing to try it? I believe this is exactly what God had in mind with the Hebrew people.

Although we are not Jewish, nor are we living in the first century, I think there are some principles to be learned from the ways that Hebrew families lived and raised children. They had a different worldview when it came to living in the culture and their role as parents. I'm not advocating that we live like a first-century Jewish family, although it might be interesting, but I believe there are some principles from family life that we can learn as we prepare to launch our children into wholeness and holiness.

It might seem a bit confusing as you hear several new terms and ideas. To make it easier to understand, you can see the basic concept in the graph below. Once we walk through a short history lesson, we will see what God's way of parenting His own people might have to say to us in the 21st century.

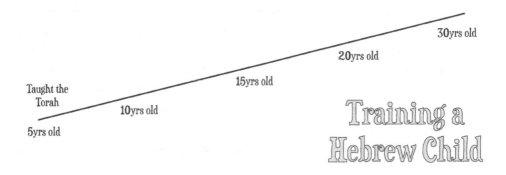

30yrs old

20yrs old

15yrs old

Taught the Torah

10yrs old

5yrs old

Training a Hebrew Child

From the age of five, a Hebrew child was beginning to learn the Torah, which is the written law of the Old Testament. In part, the children would meet with the Rabbi on a daily basis in their community, and the Rabbi would read aloud and show them the written Torah. Then they would begin to memorize it. In the Old Testament, when Scripture says "I have hidden your word in my heart that I might not sin against you" (Psalm 119:11), it was a literal practice. They believed these laws were the very words from God's mouth and looked seriously on how His words affected their lives.

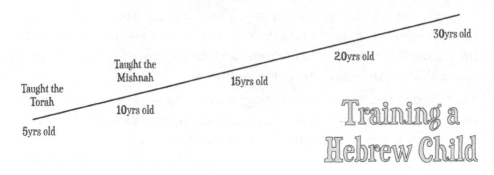

When children reached the age of ten, they began to learn the Mishnah, which is the oral interpretation of the Laws of God. Each Rabbi had their own interpretation or teaching on the Law. Many times in the New Testament, we see Jesus arguing or debating with the Pharisees and they would ask, "The Laws of Moses says this, but what do you say?" Frequently it was an argument over the Torah (written law) versus the Mishnah (oral law). For instance, the Torah may have a certain prohibition while the Mishnah could be even more restrictive. So by the age of 10, children are not just memorizing the written Law of God, but also the spoken customs of God's people as well. There would be serious spiritual teaching poured into these children before they were even teens. It's not hard to imagine the potential for life transformation.

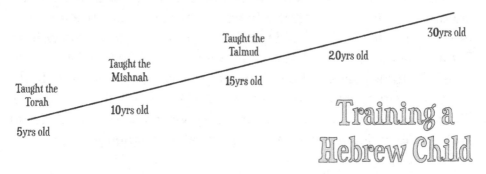

When a student approached the age of 15, he would begin to learn the Talmud. This is a collection of the civic and ceremonial laws of the Hebrew people. After learning the written law and the oral laws, these ceremonial laws would help them learn how to conduct themselves in everyday life. It brought a consistency to situations such as how to treat one another in your business, neighborhood, and marriage. On the spiritual side, the Talmud deals with complexities of various ceremonies, feasts, or festivals in the Jewish calendar. By the time students got to mid-adolescence (according to our modern-day vernacular), they had an incredible amount of knowledge and training of both Who God is and how He desired for them to live. They learned it from their "church leaders," if you want to think of it that way, but they would also learn it at home from parents and older siblings.

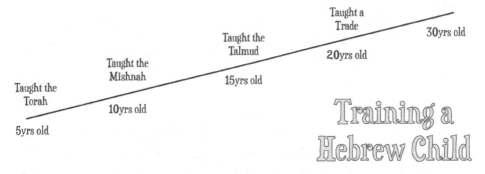

By the age of 20, a young adult would be proficient in a trade. They were essentially commissioned into a career at this point. Previously, around the age of twelve or thirteen in Hebrew "Boy School" so to speak, if you were going to make it a life goal to become a rabbi yourself, a particular rabbi would come to you and say, "Come and follow me." Those words from the rabbi meant that he would be taking the young man under his wing to be trained in that rabbi's ways and understanding of the Torah. He would be taught that Rabbi's Mishnah. In contrast, the young men who were not pursued by a rabbi would continue to train in their fathers' careers and become fishermen, farmers, and carpenters themselves. A career wasn't a haphazard undertaking. There was an intentional "intern" process put in place by the father. The father understood the weight of the task at hand to prepare his son to take over the family trade. In Luke 6:40, Jesus said, *"Students are not greater than their teacher. But the student who is fully trained will become like the teacher"*

(NLT). In the Hebrew culture, there was a great deal of respect and honor given to a teacher, in this case the fathers. Even into their twenties, young men would not be recognized in their communities as having fully arrived at maturity. They still needed to be taught.

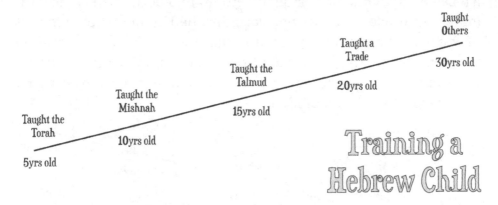

For the next ten years, young men would continue to learn a trade and live under the authority of their fathers. Around the age of thirty, they were considered fully taught and were then qualified to teach others. Who do you think it is that these "fully taught" men would begin to teach first? By the age of thirty most of them would have started their own families. The next generation of children was learning the Torah, Mishnah, and Talmud and the fathers were preparing to teach their career skills to their children. The cycle never stopped. Regardless of age, every father was in a constant state of being both a learner and a teacher.

If we compared this process to our own culture, there would be a distinct break between the ages of 18-23. Parents think of this time frame as the time that we are done with parenting and training our children. We consider them adults, help them move out, further their education, marry, and start their own families. They may come back to visit for the holidays or Sunday lunches, but for the most part, our time with them is done. But in the Hebrew culture, it is from age 20-30 that a young man would begin to spend *even more time* with his father, learning to carry on his particular craft or skill in order to carry it to the next generation. During the same time frame, they were also taught the importance of the marriage bed and how important it was to be a good husband or good wife. At this point, they were free to begin to move towards marriage. However, it wouldn't be a marriage in the way we experience it in the modern world—marrying, getting your own home, moving as far away from your parents' home as you can afford. We don't want any accidental drop-ins, right? But in the Hebrew culture, the new couple would live in an addition to the parents' home where the mentoring process could continue until the young adults had earned the right by age 30 to speak into someone else's life. This is a stark contrast to our culture where we say that by the age of 18, you are an adult and can be an authority figure on the same playing field as any other adult. It's actually quite awkward to put someone who has decades of life experience on the same level legally as an 18 year old.

Before you move on too quickly, take a moment and think about your relationship with your child in regard to the Hebrew process of parenting. Do you see any principles you might be able to apply to your own situation? Think about the influence God has given you with your child. Surely, God didn't intend for you to invest in your child's life for eighteen years, building up trust and credibility, only to shut it all down after graduation. I believe there is a different lens you could look through that will allow you not only to leverage, but also nurture the influence you have developed. Let's look at the Hebrew parent again and see how it could affect your own parenting.

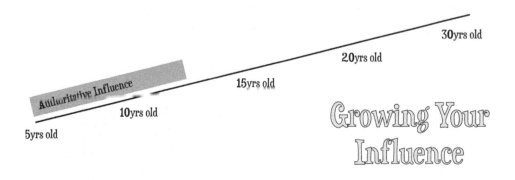

From birth until about the age of 11 or 12, you have a strong authoritative influence in the lives of your children. They look to you for directions and boundaries. Whatever rules you put in place are the law of the land without question. As long as you have been fairly consistent in the way you love and provide for your children, younger children conclude that whatever you say is generally the way of life.

You are the one who provides all of their needs. As the authority that has their best interest at heart, they look to you for comfort, protection, or assurance that all is right in the world. Ultimately, we all want our children to have their needs met through Christ, but until they are old enough to understand and know Jesus, you represent Him to them. This is why it is paramount for you to use your influence wisely as an authority. From an early age, the way they understand Jesus' love for them will be shaped by your love for them.

As chief authority in life, you are also the bearer of knowledge in the world. You are the one they trust. You know the answers. You are the one their world revolves around. Your son comes to you to ask, "Why do dogs bark at night?" Or "How come girls all wear pink?" Or best of all, "Where do babies come from?" You rack your brain for an answer by pulling from what you have learned in science, from school, and on the Discovery Channel. You might call another parent or check online, but regardless of how eloquent or lame your answer may be, your child responds with, "Oh, okay, thanks." You sweat it out hoping to say the right thing, but your child takes it for a fact that you know everything. Your children learn life from YOU, and have since before they can even remember.

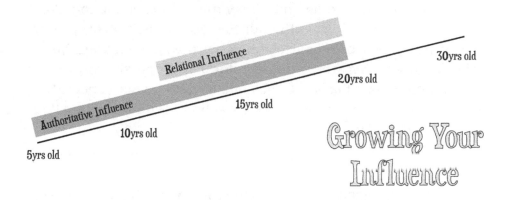

Growing Your Influence

A shift happens during early adolescence (age 12-14), when you will need to add another kind of influence—relational influence. You don't lose or set aside your authoritative influence, but you should begin to intentionally add relational influence into the mix when dealing with tweens. When a child enters early adolescence, authority is not as important to them as it once was. Relationships are what begin to drive their decision-making.

Perhaps the most contentious years in your child's life will be in middle school. No one enjoys it. Seemingly overnight everything is changing in your child's life. Their bodies are changing. Their emotions are changing. Their behavior is changing. And most troubling to you, their relationships are changing. When your young teenager's brain wakes up to life outside of your immediate family, suddenly you feel like you are competing for influence with their friendships at school, their teammates on ever-changing sports rosters, and people on Instagram you don't even know. In reality, they can't hold a flame to what you mean to your child. Friends and social media have far less influence than you may think. When a parent begins to develop relational influence in addition to the years of authoritative influence, the scales begin to tip in your favor.

I am not talking about being your child's buddy or best friend. You are still the authority figure you always were, but now you are purposefully connecting with your child in a relationship as well. An authority can make demands, but only a parent in a loving relationship can say, "Come and follow me as we live life together." You desire to walk along with your teenager to help them process and come to their own conclusions about what is just and honorable. Be aware that what you say aloud with merely your words may not hold the influence it once did. Instead, adolescents look to what your actions say about you. The actions of those around them speak much louder than words.

This shift can sometimes be difficult, especially for dads. Generally speaking, fathers in our culture are conditioned toward the authoritative influence rather than the relational influence. Because of their innate nurturing tendencies, moms are usually better able to transition to the relational influence with their teens. However, there should be a balance between both kinds of influence in the way you relate to your teens.

Let's say you get a call from your 17 year old on a Friday night at 11 o'clock. It is likely that both parents will probably respond in very predictable ways when you hear your son say, "Listen, don't get upset..." Horrible way to start a phone conversation late at night, right? Your son has had a car accident. How does a dad typically respond? "You did what? Is the car okay? Oh, I cannot even imagine how much our auto insurance is going to go up. You had better believe you'll be the one paying for that. Were you messing with your phone again? I need to call my buddy on the police force to see if we can keep it off your record." Dad is focused on figuring it all out before he even knows what happened. He is leveraging his authority. In contrast, how does mom typically respond? "Are you okay? Who was in the other car? Is anyone hurt?" She is instantly concerned about the relationships, the people involved, and the emotional impact. This doesn't mean that Mom is not worried about the broken boundaries, the details of the accident, or the ramifications of future consequences. She will certainly find out tomorrow morning about the rainy streets, the missed curfew, and the extra passenger that should never have been riding in the car with her son in the first place. But in the immediate circumstance, the relational details come into play. Dads can learn to balance both types of influence by communicating their willingness to come alongside a teen with wisdom and emotional support in crisis moments. Likewise, mothers can sometimes be guilty of sacrificing the authority influence altogether while trying to get their teen to approve of them or be their friend. This tendency would need to be balanced to ensure an appropriate level of respect. There should always be a healthy tension between your relational and authoritative influence.

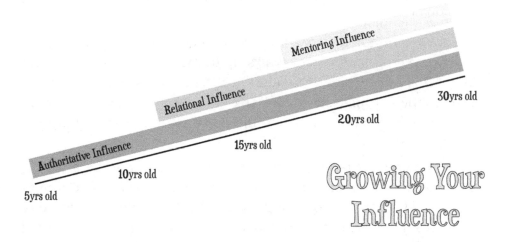

Mentoring Influence

Relational Influence

30yrs old

20yrs old

Authoritative Influence

15yrs old

10yrs old

5yrs old

Growing Your Influence

As your teen gets older and eases into adulthood, you will still be an authority, you will still walk alongside them as a relational influence, but you will also become a coach to them. At some point, your role changes from merely a teacher to that of a mentor or advisor. This role is all about modeling the daily faithfulness of a walk with Christ. If you have a child who has graduated from high school or college, moved out of your home, or maybe just gotten married, you inevitably have begun to be confronted with your own mortality. You are keenly aware that you have a limited amount of time left. My wife and I were having a conversation about this in the car not long ago. I said something like, "Now that we are about a third of the way through our lives, what's the next phase going to look like for us?" After overhearing the comment (and apparently doing the math), my very literal son pipes in from the back seat, "Dad, you're 45. Statistically, you're more than halfway done." Whoa. How is that for that a shock back into reality? It is not very likely that I will live to be 100. Seeing my children go through high school makes me aware that I only have a certain amount of time left, and I want to use the time wisely.

I was at a church recently leading one of our "Leaving a Spiritual Legacy" sessions. It is always a powerful time with a local church speaking into families about the legacy that their lives can leave. We are fifteen minutes away from the service starting when there is a loud crash against the back door leading into the auditorium. The next several minutes were a whirlwind of activity as people went to investigate. The lead pastor walks up to me five minutes later and says, "One of our older members just had a massive heart attack in the lobby and passed away." The amazing thing was what happened next. No one was panicked. People weren't running around unsure of what to do next.

As paramedics tended to this gentleman, one person after another began to tell stories about him. One woman said, "Every Sunday, he told me what a blessing I was." Another said, "He was one of the best fathers I knew." Still another, "Did you know Mr. C read through the entire Bible every year?" I never had the pleasure of meeting him, but as person after person told stories about him it was obvious that he used his time wisely to leave a spiritual legacy with his life. He had no idea that this day would be the end of his own race. But as he crossed the finished line, he was able to offer to Christ the gift of a family of fully devoted followers, which he had spent a lifetime raising up.

Once your child reaches a certain age, you are no longer as concerned about being an authority in your child's life. You are not thinking about how to manage your 25-year-old son's time or how to make sure your 29 year old is making wise choices when it comes to her career, because you know she has it well under control. Instead, you are more concerned with the question, "Who am I as a person and what do I believe as a child of God is most important for me to pass down to the next generation?" If I only have a limited amount of time with my children, what do I want to pass on to them? This is transformational influence. It is during this phase that you begin to invite your nearly grown children (from ages 16 to 30) into some of your specific life experiences.

You could plan mission work for part of a summer where you spend time serving together so your older teens get to see you living out your faith in a different way. Maybe you invite your teen into your career in some way so she sees firsthand what you do and begins to understand what God has equipped you to accomplish. Perhaps, instead of loading a typical small group for your adult peer group, you start an inter-generational small group so your teens can experience community with both their own peers and older adults. You begin to treat them more as peers than as children. Your teen may not have the same level of life experience yet, but you are beginning to go to the same place spiritually and relationally together. When the time is appropriate, you will speak truth. As necessary, you may need to be brutally honest about blind spots in your teen's life. You also recognize that your young adult is likely to be far more deeply impacted by being invited into what God is doing in your blind spots, than for you to point out theirs.

During the last five years of my dad's life, I got to spend time with him painting houses every so often. For about the last decade of his life, he went to work for himself as a painter and handyman. Whenever he needed an extra man for an odd week during the summer, he would give me a call. So I got to help him in what he did for a living. Instead of defaulting to my own schedule of ministry responsibilities, camps, and speaking engagements and telling him that I could not really justify the time away, I felt that the Lord was prompting me to make the time to work with my dad. I needed to do it even if it took time away from my plans for the summer. I hated every minute that I had to paint those houses. I don't know anyone who actually enjoys painting outside during the heat of summer. My dad called it "chasing the shade" when we would move the ladders and supplies to whichever side of the house was out of direct sunlight. But those two weeks each summer with my dad were moments I will never regret.

The one thing I cherished about those two summers was seeing my father in a very different role. Since I was almost 40 years old by that time and my dad was in his mid-60s, I wasn't a boy or even a young adult just starting out trying to figure life out on my own. Instead I was an adult who could see my dad as another man of faith following Christ just like I was. At some point each year, we all spent time with him that way—my brother, his wife, my wife, our teens—watching him paint, assisting him however we could, and listening to his stories.

When we were one on one, I found myself asking him relationship questions like, "Hey, Dad, what was it like the first time you saw Mom? Where did you go on your first date?" I also asked him deeper questions like, "What's the one thing you wish you never struggled with," and "Why did you finally decide to give your life to Christ?" I was about 13 when he became a Christian, so I had a memory of how he was before and after. I wondered what one or two key things God had shown him that he never wanted to forget. I had no idea that by the end of that last summer, my dad would pass away from a sudden heart attack. I am so grateful for those times we had together just the two of us when my dad was a mentoring influence in my life. As I grew up, my Dad had struggled to adapt and figure out what his role was supposed to be in my brother's life and mine. Towards the end, however, he was able to let God mold him to be a godly authority, a faithful friend, and a wise mentor.

If your child is in their late teens or early 20s, I encourage you to stop and give yourself time to think through what your child might really need from you right now. None of us are going to be perfect in this phase. None of our kids are either. They may still fail to stick to schedules and never have quite learned to keep their rooms clean. They may even have a moral failure to deal with that has serious, long-term consequences. But take a look at the big picture. Where are they in life and what do they need from you? Does each of your children believe who God says they are? Are they in places of rebellion, lostness, confusion, stability, or peace? Are they a prodigal son or a praised son? Does your nearly adult child need you to acknowledge that while her friends seem to be falling by the wayside or moving on without her, you are not going anywhere? You are in it with her. She is never alone, never abandoned. Pray for the Lord to give you insight into how you can live out the kind of influence God desires for you to have in your older child's life. Likewise, pray for your children to have hearts that are teachable and open to being led by you.

Earlier in the chapter, I mentioned Luke 6:40 when Jesus said, *"Students are not greater than their teacher. But the student who is fully trained will become like the teacher"* (NLT). In the next verse, Jesus talks about getting the log out of your own eye instead of focusing on the speck in someone else's eye. It is easy to look at the passage and see it as a commentary on judging others. What Jesus is actually talking about is the difference between a heart rooted in humility versus a heart filled with arrogance. Jesus shows what happens when we have a prideful heart and think we are above someone else speaking into our lives. At times, we all are guilty of thinking we have the whole thing figured out to such an extent that we can now tell someone else what is wrong with their life. That is a bit like what our culture does for an 18 year old on a regular basis. It tells them, "You're grown. You're on your own. Nobody can tell you what to do." Soon after, they crash and burn. Instead, Jesus says there should always be a teacher and a student. While we hope for a willingly responsive heart from our children, we must remember as parents that we, too, are under authority.

Our culture today teaches that when you turn eighteen, you are your own person and no longer under your parents' authority. If we again look to the first century Jewish family as a model, however, we would see that this was far from the life they embraced. Let's say you are between the ages of 18-20 years old. You have gotten married, learned a trade, and are well on your way to becoming an authority figure in your own right. At what point would you no longer be under your parents' authority? When you start your own business? Maybe when you have your own children? Perhaps on your tenth anniversary? In reality, even as an accomplished, well-balanced adult, you would view yourself as being under their authority until they died. Their authority in your life would always be present, acknowledged, and accepted.

This is the mindset of humility that Jesus tried to instill in His followers. None of us has the whole thing figured out. Until Jesus comes back again, we will not be fully like our teacher. We are all still in process...including parents. We are still in process as slaves to Christ and children to our own parents. Some of us may even need to make things right with aging parents before trying to work things out with our children. Just as we desire a teachable heart from our children, God desires the same teachable spirit toward our own parents. Always learning while also leading.

Conclusion

Several years ago my friend Coby took me on a mountain hike outside Portland, Oregon. We walked a couple of miles up a narrow path that crisscrossed one side of the mountain. The beauty surrounding us was begging for a crowd to see it, but we were more than glad to have the experience all to ourselves.

As we crested another ridge that looked like every other ridge we had topped, Coby quietly said, "Look at that." There in front of us sitting in perfect serenity was the unexpected treasure of a mountain lake. Taking a few steps closer toward the water's edge, all conversation stopped. We sat in silence taking in a holy moment, seeing some of the best of what God had made. Neither of us had to speak to know it was a gift.

As inspiring as the moment was, no guy can sit still in front of a perfectly calm lake for too long. There is something in us, I am sure put there by our Creator, that yearns to leave a mark everywhere we go. Without saying a word, we both knew what needed to be done as we felt the gravelly surface beneath our hiking boots—it was the perfect time to skip some rocks.

You may remember learning to skip a rock in a creek or pond when you were growing up. There is something empowering about breaking up the glassy shimmer of the sun's reflection off the water with nothing more than a small smooth stone. The natural order of things is interrupted as the rock exerts its will on the water. The flat stone will soon meet its fate at the bottom of the pond, but not before it leaves its mark on the surface. The weight of the rock's influence doesn't stop with one splash. Each distinct hop of the rock causes a separate set of concentric circles to form in the water.

Coby and I sat in the rough grass talking about our families as we flung rock after rock across the water. We talked about his little ones learning to walk and mine learning Algebra. His had not taken the training wheels off their bikes yet, and mine were looking forward to a driver's permit. Though they will be years apart, there will come a day that each of our children will open the front door, walk out, and not consider our home the place they lay their head to rest any longer. Our children were in very different seasons of life, but we talked as men who wanted to soak up every experience to the fullest.

The most fascinating part about skipping a rock across the water is watching what happens after the initial splash. The one circle becomes two, then three, then four, and on and on. Some of the rocks we skipped caused circles to continue so far across the lake that we couldn't see them any longer.

After you spend more than two decades parenting, the hope is that our children will make an impact for God's kingdom far beyond anything we can see. I take hope in knowing that their Heavenly Father's dreams for their lives are far grander, generous, and rewarding than anything you or I could fathom. Whether your children are as young as Coby's or nearing college like mine, we must all acknowledge that our days are numbered. The choices you make with them now are setting them up to make one splash after another for God's glory. It is time to fling some spiritual rocks across the waters and see what God has in store.

Let Them Venture, but Prepare for the Return Trip

Imagine that you are holding a big rubber band. Better yet, go grab one from your junk drawer. With very little effort, the band stretches when you handle it a little. The more you pull it back, the further out of shape it gets. But the moment you let it go, it pops back to its original shape and form. It does not matter how small or large the rubber band is, it will stretch to a certain extent and then come back to the original form. The same thing is true of your children. If you have an understanding of your changing roles through-out their lives, then you don't have to be afraid when your kids be-gin to pull away at eighteen thinking they are ready to be their own person, blaze their own trail, and live their own life. At that time, you can say, "You belong to the Lord, not to me. And because I have walked with you these last eighteen years, I've modeled for you and taught you Christlikeness, and I've shown you wholeness and holiness, I can entrust you to His hands." At that point, there will certainly be times that your son or daughter will pull away, but he or she will snap back. The bond you have spent years creating will be too strong for distance, time, or career to break.

On April 12, 1961, Russian Cosmonaut Yuri Gagarin became the first human in outer space[1]. His experience in orbit was years in the making, yet his time in orbit was only 108 minutes. Can you imag-ine spending years working toward something that only lasted an hour and a half? Things changed in 2000 with the commissioning of the International Space Station. Since then, the longest single spaceflight by a woman is by American Astronaut Sunita Williams at 195 days. Over the course of six different flights, Russian Cosmo-naut Sergei Avdeyev spent more than 803 days in space. That's over two years of his life...in space! Even though science and engineer-ing has allowed man to spend longer periods of time in space, at the end of every mission the astronauts come back to Earth. They snap back just like the rubber band returns to its original shape; just like your child returns home.

Your adult child's relationship with you is like home base. God has wired them for independence and their own identity; therefore, they will explore the world and taste the wild blue yonder, but they will always come back. They will return when they need your help. They will come back when they need your influence. When they need your words and your advice, they will come back again. There will be times when they venture away and end up making four dif-ferent decisions about four different majors in college or four dif-ferent jobs. They may change from working with computers to car-pentry to real estate to ministry. Part of our job as parents is not to manage our children. Instead we must encourage our children to live out truth and godliness themselves until they discover the personality and giftedness that God has given them, knowing that the rubber band is always going to snap back.

Colossians 3:20 says, *"Children, obey your parents in everything, for this pleases the Lord."* Ephesians 6:1-2 says, *"Children, obey your parents because you belong to the Lord, for this is the right thing to do. Honor your father and mother"* (NLT). When we see those Scriptures, we think that's what my child is supposed to do—honor me. Listen to me, obey me, and do what I say. All of that is true. However, when Paul writes these words to the churches at Colossi and Ephesus, how old are the children he is writing to? He is talking to anyone with a parent who is still alive. Right? *Our* parents have had to experience the rubber band effect as they watched us move out from under their care. There have been times when you have walked away from your parents or moved because of a career change or marriage. Then you came back. You pulled away again when you started a family, but when you wanted your children to get to know their grandparents, you came back. You moved away during a time of career advancement and promotion, but came back when you lost your job. That is how God designed things.

Consider that the biggest obstacle to your child becoming who God created them to be might be you. Fear can become immobilizing. When you let your mind wander into the unknown—the place where God hasn't given clear answers yet—it is easy to feel out of control. You fear for your child's future and safety. You fear whether or not they can take care of themselves. You fear their strength and ability to know truth. The list goes on and on. If you are unwilling to open the door and trust that God has your child's best interest at heart, they may never get to prove they can trust God themselves. Culture-shaper Shane Claiborne said, *"Family is one of the most significant barriers to potential risk takers who would leave everything for the way of the cross."*[2] Don't let it be said that your child's legacy was shortchanged because you could not see that God is much bigger than all of life's unknowns.

Celebrate Their Successes and Grieve Their Disappointments

As your children grow into independence and self-awareness, you are still part of every success and disappointment of their lives. You get to be their biggest cheerleader, pushing them on from the sidelines and championing their causes with your words and prayers. Other times you have the privilege of being a counselor and priest when they go through crushing disappointments. Regardless of the experience, you must always be aware of the ultimate Author of their story. Just as you have done all along, point them back to the One who plans their path. Help them to give God the glory when things go well and to cling to Him during sorrow.

The real tragedy in being a helicopter parent who hovers over every move a child makes is not that the child never learns self-reliance or responsibility. It's that when the child has a major breakthrough, guess who gets credit for success. The parent. You got them the job. You got them the recommendation. You pulled the strings to get them where they are. In the end, you get the credit for who your adult child is. Instead, if you allow God to do His work in your child's life, when there is a success, your whole family can say, "Wow. Look at what God did." Instead of celebrating what you did, you get to celebrate God's goodness and blessing in their life.

Likewise, in the times when there are failures, you can come alongside your adult children in their disappointment and bear the burden with them. You don't have to fix the situation, but you can walk with them as God makes a way clear to them. You get to be part of the growing process in their lives as they learn to depend on Him to be their provider, their protector, and their deliverer. You can release them, for better or worse, as God uses their success to push them to further heights for His glory and show them the way to hope and peace through their failures.

Pass on the Blessing to Your Child

There is nothing more freeing and emboldening to a child than receiving a blessing from their parent. Likewise, nothing is more paralyzing and stunting to a child's development than never receiving a parent's blessing. A blessing is a proclamation to your son that he is a man and to your daughter that she has become a woman. You no longer see them as merely your child. Now they are sojourners with you. You are fully partners in a spiritual journey together.

A parent's blessing doesn't have to happen at a particular age, but can be a transformational moment if done during a significant life transition. It can be when your children graduate, get married, or start a new job. The blessing is simply whenever you are able to find a specific moment of time to stand before your child and look them in the eye to say something along the lines that, "You and me, we're okay. No matter where you go or what you do, I've got your back. And I pray that the God who made you will do things in you that are beyond your expectations and imagination. Everything I am as your parent, I have passed down to you. Now it's time for you to live those same truths for the next generation. We have honored the Lord before you and alongside you. Now you go and honor Him."

There is a story in the book of Numbers when God speaks to Moses about a blessing for His people. He instructs Moses to tell Aaron and his sons to bless the people of Israel with this special blessing:

> "May the LORD bless you and protect you,
> May the LORD smile on you and be gracious to you.
> May the LORD show you his favor and give you his
> peace" (Numbers 6:24-26; NLT).

There are two things in this story that blow my mind. One, God doesn't need Aaron's help. God is plenty big enough to handle blessing His people on His own. Yet, God tells Aaron and his sons to give this blessing from Him. It's as if God were waiting for us to finish the process. We ask God to bless our children, to show Himself, to give His provision, and to show His favor in our children's lives. I wonder if the reason why they don't feel God's blessing and favor is that we have yet to do our part to partner with God? We haven't spoken those words into them. In order for your child to be aware of God's blessing, you must speak it into them.

In the Jewish culture, there was a moment in time when the patriarch would stand before his son in the midst of his family and lay hands on the son as a symbol that the father's name and authority was being passed down to the next generation. Abraham laid his hands on Isaac in blessing. Years later, Isaac would bless Jacob, and then Jacob would bless his son Joseph. This same blessing passed from generation to generation is yours to pass on as well. You, too, can have the same opportunity. Find that moment in your own family when you stand before your grown child to pass the baton of wholeness and holiness.

The second amazing thing that occurs in the story with Aaron is what happens after the blessing. In Numbers 6:27 God says, "Whenever Aaron and his sons bless the people of Israel in my name, I myself will bless them" (NLT). God says He will not only bless the people, but He will also bless the one who is passing on the blessing to His people.

When you pass the blessing to your children, you in turn receive a blessing from the Lord. You may be just now starting the spiritual journey with your little ones. Or maybe you are the parent whose children are older and you are keenly aware of the limited number of days you have left with them. Regardless of where you are in your relationship with your child, there is a promise you can cling to. There is a promise that makes all of the sleepless nights, skinned knees, back-talking, financial sacrifices, long road trips, and the 2,587 sack lunches you made worth it. As you are giving the blessing, you too will receive a blessing. He will bless you and watch over you. He will smile over you and shower you with grace. He will give you His favor and you will know His peace. There is no greater reward that you could ask for.

Endnotes

Introduction
[1] http://www.mtv.com/thinkmtv/research

Chapter One
[1] http://www.reaganfoundation.org/reagan/nancy/just_say_no.asp

Chapter Three
[1] http://en.wikipedia.org/wiki/Dan_O'Brien. You can go to YouTube to see the iconic commercials that Nike in Dan's first failed attempt to make it to the Olympics.

Chapter Four
[1] Copyright © 1998 worshiptogether.com Songs (ASCAP) sixsteps Music (ASCAP) (adm. at CapitolCMGPublishing.com) All rights reserved. Used by permission.

[2] There are actually many online sources discussing the "hook up" culture. Here are a couple to get you started. http://theweek.com/articles/498717/love-time-hooking and http://articles.latimes.com/2013/aug/12/local/la-me-hooking-up-20130813. To read some of the scientific data, read "The Shift from Dating to Hooking Up In College: What Scholars Have Missed," Sociology Compass, October 2007, Volume 10, pp 775-788 by Kathleen A. Bogle and "To Hook Up or Date: Which Gender Benefits?" Sex Roles, May 2010, Volume 62, Issue 9-10, pp 661-669 by Bradshaw et al.

[3] To understand more about the trends concerning underage children lying on social media check out http://www.northwestern.edu/newscenter/stories/2011/10/hargittai-facebook-underage.html and http://www.theguardian.com/media/2013/jul/26/children-lie-age-facebookasa.

Chapter Five
[1] The Effective Christian Education: A National Study of Protestant Congregations was conducted by Search Institute in 1990 by interviewing over 11,000 teenagers from 561 congregations. As a disclaimer, even though this study

was extensive among Christian teenagers, no teens in the Southern Baptist Denomination were interviewed. The SBC tends to be more conservative than a few of the others that were included in the study. I have to wonder if this would have changed any of the results. Nonetheless, it is well worth seeing how teenagers feel about the role of church, family, and faith in their lives. You can find more on this study at http://stickyfaith.org.

Chapter Six

[1] http://abcnews.go.com/Technology/angie-varona-14-year-unwillingly-internet-sex-symbol/story?id=14882768.

[2] I'm sure you know most of these stories already, but it is an interesting study when you compare what happened to each of these people after being up on a mountaintop with God. To check it out yourself, look up each of their experiences: Matthew 17:1, Genesis 8:15, Exodus 34:1, and 1 Kings 18:19.

[3] This is one of the most repeated words of advice about parenting that came from a radio show that Josh McDowell did on Focus on the Family on October 16, 1987.

Chapter Seven

[1] For a synopsis of this research from the Barna Group see https://www.barna.org/teens-nextgen-articles/528-six-reasons-young-christians-leave-church. For a more thorough understanding of the mind of this generation of teens and young concerning their religious beliefs and feeling on the church pick up a copy of You Lost Me: Why Young Christian Are Leaving Church and Rethinking Faith (Baker Books, 2011) by David Kinnaman. If we are going to foster a lasting faith in the next generation of Christ followers, then we are going to have to start implementing some of the practices Kinnaman recommends.

[2] The extensive results of the study were published in the book Sticky Faith: Everyday Ideas to Build Lasting Faith in Your Kids (Zondervan, 2011). This book by Dr. Kara Powell and Dr. Chap Clark should be on your short list of books to pick up. It is both sobering and encouraging as you read the first-hand stories of students trying to process what their faith means to them.

Chapter Eight

[1] http://www.nytimes.com/1982/10/12/science/newborns-found-able-to-imitate-facialexpressions.

html. Just for kicks if you want to understand more about the fascinating wonder of the science of infancy, check out Baby Meets World by Nicholas Day.

[2] http://yaledailynews.com/blog/2007/12/06/study-children-over-imitate-adults/

[3] Parent and Child Cigarette Use: A Longitudinal, Multigenerational Study. Mike Viola and Jeremy Staff. Purdue University. http://www.purdue.edu/newsroom/releases/2013/Q3/studyteens-smoking-influenced-by-older-siblings,-parents-lifelong-smoking-habits.html. For further study see: Changes in Friends' and Parental Influences on Cigarette Smoking From Early Through Late Adolescence. Yue Liao, Zhaoqing Huang, Jimi Huh , Mary Ann Pentz , Chih-Ping Chou. Adolescent Health, 2013.

[4] 2010 Teen Survey. The National Center on Addition and Substance Abuse (CASA) at Columbia University. CASA has been conducting the most extensive yearly surveys on teen trends concerning drugs, alcohol, sexuality, and bullying for twenty years.

Conclusion

[1] http://en.wikipedia.org/wiki/Yuri_Gagarin

[2] If you have a teenager, The Irresistible Revolution: Living as an Ordinary Radical (Zondervan, 2009) by Shane Claiborne should be required reading. Shane's stories of living the gospel among "the least of these" will inspire both you and your teenager to view living the gospel and living in community differently.

About the Author

Brian is a prolific writer for parenting magazines, most notably *Parenting Teenagers* and *Parent Life.* He publishes two blogs, "Conversations on Napkin" and "Tech Savvy Parenting." He is also the author of *Engaging Your Teen's World* and *Tech Savvy Parenting.*

Brian and his wife, Mona, have been married for twenty-one years and have two teenagers of their own: a son, Bailey, and daughter, Ashlan. Besides loving and shaping their own teens, together they enjoy coaching other parents. Brian has served families for more than twenty-two years in a variety of positions including youth pastor, school administrator, teaching pastor, and camp director. Brian serves as the executive director for 360 Family, a nonprofit dedicated to encouraging and equipping parents to understand their teenagers, based in Memphis, TN.

Brian has had the privilege of speaking at more than 100 conferences and countless churches, schools, camps, and military bases. He has led student and parent programs from coast to coast as well as several international locations.

Interested in having Brian speak at your PTA/PTF, church group, parent conferences, or family camp? Visit www.360family.org for more information.

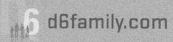

What is **D6?**

BASED ON DEUTERONOMY 6:4-7

A **conference** for your entire **team**

A **curriculum** for every age at **church**

An **experience** for every person in your **home**

Connecting
CHURCH & HOME
These must work together!

D6 CONFERENCE
ONCE A YEAR

DEFINE & REFINE Your Discipleship Plan

www.d6family.com

ONE HOUR A WEEK

POWER OF
PARENTAL INFLUENCE

CPSIA information can be obtained
at www.ICGtesting.com
Printed in the USA
LVHW081921110819
626989LV00010B/6/P